CHIRU SAKURA

Caitlin Press Inc.
8100 Alderwood Road
Halfmoon Bay, BC VoN 1Y1
www.caitlin-press.com

Edited by Meg Yamamoto
Printed in Canada
Cover design by Vici Johnstone

Caitlin Press Inc. acknowledges financial support from the Government of Canada and the Canada Council for the Arts, and the Province of British Columbia through the British Columbia Arts Council and the Book Publisher's Tax Credit.

Library and Archives Canada Cataloguing in Publication

Chiru sakura — falling cherry blossoms : a mother & daughter's journey through racism, internment and oppression / Grace Eiko Thomson ; edited by Meg Yamamoto.

Falling cherry blossoms | Mother & daughter's journey through racism, internment and oppression | Mother and daughter's journey through racism, internment and oppression

Thomson, Grace Eiko, author. | Yamamoto, Meg, editor.

Canadiana 20200408917 | ISBN 9781773860411 (softcover)
LCSH: Thomson, Grace Eiko. | LCSH: Thomson, Grace Eiko—Family. | CSH: Japanese Canadians—Biography.|
    CSH: Japanese Canadians—Evacuation and relocation, 1942-1945. | CSH: Japanese Canadians—Social conditions. |
    LCSH: Mothers and daughters—Canada—Biography. | LCSH: Canada—Race relations. | LCGFT: Autobiographies.
LCC FC106.J3 Z7 2021 | DDC 971/.0049560092—dc23

Chiru Sakura

Falling Cherry Blossoms

A Mother and Daughter's Journey through
Racism, Internment and Oppression

GRACE EIKO THOMSOM

CAITLIN PRESS 2021

Before beginning this journey, I acknowledge that we are living on unceded xʷməθkʷəy̓əm (Musqueam), Sḵwx̱wú7mesh (Squamish) and səl̓ílwətaʔɬ/ Selilwitulh (Tsleil-Waututh) territories.

To my family members and friends

In memory of my parents, Sawae and Torasaburo Nishikihama

CONTENTS

Grace visiting her mother, Sawae, in her mother's home in Vancouver, c. 1980.
Author's personal collection

INTRODUCTION

Mother begins:

March 1, 1997

I am currently living in a senior care residence, passing my every day in gratitude for the care and support given me by my son Kenji and daughters Eiko and Keiko. Gradually, I seem to be losing my memory, so I have been making note of things I want to leave behind, such as how I have been spending my time and what I experienced, especially during the Second World War.

I am now eighty-four years of age.

One day, while I was visiting my mother at the care home where she was residing, she offered me a small green booklet titled "Journal." Pointing to the opening page, she said, "Here, take a look. Can you read this?" It appeared to be a diary, beginning with the date March 1, 1997. I read the first page out loud to her. She smiled and said, "Oh, that's good. I'll keep it at that level," and quickly withdrew the book.

I wondered at the time what that was all about. She did not explain it to me, but of course she was confirming that I could read her entries, which were written in Japanese. What I had seen was the beginning page of a memoir that she would eventually leave with me to translate and to share with my siblings.

When she handed the booklet back to me a few years later, saying "It's finished" and nothing more, for some reason, likely because she was still near me in my daily life, I did not act immediately. I read the booklet over quickly and then, even as questions arose in my mind, I put it aside. (Was I avoiding the past? Yes, I think so.)

It wasn't until a few years later, when Mother was experiencing health problems, that I began thinking of our past together. Once I realized that I was nearing the age at which she had begun writing her memoir, I felt an urgency not only to read it again but also to examine my own memories of the years I had spent with her as a child and a young woman, often in conflict, as between a strong mother born in Japan and a stubborn, though always obedient, daughter born here in Canada. Ours was a complicated relationship during difficult times.

In the spring of 2001, with a fracture in her back caused by osteoporosis, Mother had been admitted to Mount Saint Joseph Hospital in Vancouver to receive treatment for pain control and rehabilitation. She was at that time living in Adanac Towers, the Kinsmen apartment for seniors on Commercial Drive, where several other seniors of Japanese ancestry resided.

During the month she was confined, the younger of her two sons, my brother Kenji, who had been suffering from lung cancer, died. Though she tried, and even got dressed to go to the funeral service, Mother did not have the strength to attend. Since her older son, my brother Toyoaki, and her husband, my father, Torasaburo, had passed in 1983 and 1985, respectively, Kenji had been her sole caregiver before my move back to Vancouver in 1994. Very kind and thoughtful, Kenji had phoned Mother daily, offering the news and a weather forecast, including advice on whether to venture outdoors or not.

After leaving the hospital, Mother tried to maintain her apartment but within days she had fallen off her bed and had to be returned to hospital care. An independent woman, she had lain on the floor until morning, not wishing to bother anyone during the night. She announced to me from her hospital bed that she had no intention of returning to her apartment but would await a room in a care facility. As luck would have it, she was soon notified of a space opening at the German-Canadian Care Home. She clearly declared her intention: "I will go there. I remember visiting someone at that home and I thought it was a good place."

Unlike other seniors I had heard about, who had to be persuaded to move to such a facility for their own sake, Mother instructed me to immediately begin clearing out her apartment, saying she had no need or desire to go back there and enumerating only a few things to be kept.

When my sister Keiko came from her home in Winnipeg to help in the process, Mother instructed us from her bed, "Don't forget to go through the things on the balcony. Take the planters apart, and dispose of them carefully."

We wondered what in the world she was talking about. Who cared about planters on the balcony when she was leaving the apartment? But when mothers instruct, though we may often argue, we usually obey. And in doing so, we were aghast to find, tucked in a plastic bag in one of the planters, bills totalling $10,000! She told us after we found the money that the cash had been kept there for emergency purposes and now we should use it as required.

Because of the way Mother had prepared for this eventuality, Keiko and I felt no need for sadness about her move. In fact, there was some hilarity not only about the hidden money but also over other things we joked about admiringly with family members. For instance, in going through Mother's personal belongings, we found attached to each piece of jewellery or valuable object a note specifying who should have it, or where the item had come from and who had given it to her so that we might return it to the original owner.

Upon moving into the care home, she had adjusted in short order. Whenever I visited, I saw that she was receiving hugs from staff members, especially the younger ones. I felt great relief at seeing this since I had some guilt about not inviting her to live with me. Mother and I had discussed this briefly and had agreed laughingly that we would be arguing in no time. More than that, I was living at the time in North Vancouver and commuting to a job at the Burnaby Art Gallery.

I phoned Mother daily to ensure she was all right, and we met weekly for a meal or more often as needs arose.

I did have one particular worry, and that was about the food served at the German-Canadian home. I thought that Mother would miss eating Japanese food, her own cooking, but she seemed not at all concerned with the menu. In fact, one time when I took her to Hi Gen-ki restaurant at Nikkei Place in Burnaby, she commented that the rice there was *kowai* (not cooked to her taste). I suspected it was not about the rice. I had taken her to consider an apartment at Sakura-so, the seniors' residence at Nikkei Place, since one of her friends, Mrs. Hara, lived there. But Mother found the apartment she toured too large, especially since it contained a washer, a dryer and a stove, all, she said, things of her past that she had no use for now. A few weeks after our visit, we learned that, sadly for Mother, her friend Mrs. Hara had quite suddenly passed away.

We continued with our weekly lunch at a sushi restaurant on Commercial Drive, not far from her new home, enjoying the *nabeyaki*, *donburi*, sushi and sashimi. I think that was quite enough Japanese food for her. In fact, our family had always eaten Western food, perhaps even more than Japanese food, in our everyday lives. Father, having lived and worked in Canada for some years before he married, including particularly at railway hotels, enjoyed Western food and loved to cook. He introduced us to various dishes.

Mother was, I believe, as I am today, quite content with solitude, her own company. She was always busy reading and writing. After moving to the home, she took to watching drama series on TV, likely owing to her failing eyesight, which prevented heavy reading. She would at times talk to me about something someone had done, only for me to realize later that the person was a character in a soap opera she had been watching. This led me to wonder how much English she actually understood. I had never heard her speak more than a few necessary words, and she relied on me entirely as her interpreter—so I had thought.

At times she would complain about something that was not in accord with or done to her satisfaction at the home. But when I suggested that I bring the matter up with staff, she would say, "No, don't. I can handle this on my own." Of course, I worried about how she was going to do this. When Keiko and I emptied Mother's suite at the care home after her passing in 2002, we found on her desk many scraps of paper on which were written Japanese words or phrases with the English equivalents beside them, likely taken from the many dictionaries Father had left behind. She was a proud woman and insisted on managing on her own.

I did not begin translating her memoir until after she passed. And it was in rereading it that I began realizing how generational differences affect interpretation of those years, the many years of struggle each of us, together and apart, had lived and endured. I decided then to complete the journey begun by Mother, each of us finding our own resolution.

PART ONE

The author's maternal grandparents, Fukumatsu and Ei Yamamoto in Japan. Photo taken by S. Tashima, Matsuaecho Studio, Yokohama. Author's personal collection

ORIGINS

In her memoir, Mother (Yamamoto Sawae) describes her background as follows (names are always spoken and written with the surname first in Japanese culture):

> I was born the second daughter of Yamamoto Fukumatsu and Shioji Ei of the village of Mio, today known as Mihama City, in Wakayama Prefecture, on January 14, 1913. Just a year later, my younger sister, Hideyo, was born and my father requested one of my mother's sisters to take care of us. My mother was not from Mio but from Inami, five *ri* [twenty kilometres; one *ri* equals four kilometres] from Mio, and she often went back to her home village to visit her parents. Whenever she was away, I was looked after by an aunt Nishi. I remember many mornings waking and calling out for my mother and finding that she was away again, and I would be in tears, and it was Sashi-ba [Aunt Sashi] who came to comfort me.
>
> In 1920, when I was seven years old, I entered the Mio elementary school, and after six years I went on to complete the junior high level.
>
> I had a sister three years older and this sister was always getting the first-prize book award, and I would receive awards in specific subjects, such as ethics and arithmetic. Throughout, until I finished the sixth year and junior high, I received the *suzuri* or *tachi-kami* [awards].
>
> My mother bore three daughters, no sons, and received much criticism for this, but she was very proud and happy at each year's graduation ceremony in March when each of her daughters came home with prizes.

After junior high school, I was sent to a school of good housekeeping in the village of Hiisaki. Together with three or four classmates, carrying *obentō* [packed lunch] on our hips, we climbed over Ubuyu Hill and, passing through the village of Ubuyu and over Hiisaki's hill, arrived each morning at the school. After school, I went to a teacher's home to learn *chadō* [tea ceremony] and *ikebana* [flower arrangement]. This is how I spent the year.

About this time, a good-housekeeping school came to be established in Mio, so I transferred to this school in my home village. The ikebana teacher came from Hiisaki to teach us once a week.

After I completed two years, my mother took me the following year to Wakayama City to study sewing, while living with relatives. Being left in this strange place, when my mother left, I remember feeling very lonely. Innocent about life, I had finally accustomed myself to my new life when, just after a little more than a year had passed, word came that my mother had become ill, so I returned home. The three daughters cared for her, but despite our efforts, she passed away. That was when I was seventeen years of age.

In accordance with my father's wishes, I was then sent to live with one of my father's distant relatives. The "adoption" agreement was with a couple who had never met me, and I am someone who has my mother's blood flowing through me. They had never had any children of their own, and upon my arrival they seemed to be content with this new arrangement, but this was a brief moment of peace.

I rarely heard Mother speak about her parents while we were growing up. Likely that was because her mother had died prior to her marriage, and her father died soon after she immigrated to Canada. It may also have been because traditionally in Japan, once a woman is married, it is the husband's family that takes precedence over her own.

It was only within the last ten years or so before Mother died that I

Sawae at seventeen. She was studying in Wakayama when her mother became sick, and Sawae returned to care for her before her passing. Author's personal collection

learned from her some interesting facts about her parents. Her life before Canada was quite different from what I had construed in my imagination.

I learned, for instance, that she and her two sisters were products of their father's second marriage. Our family album contains a photograph of my grandparents, Fukumatsu Yamamoto and Ei Shioji, taken in a Yokohama studio, likely at the time they were married.

Fukumatsu was a younger son, so he had no chance of any family inheritance. For that reason, he was sent to a Yamamoto family (I don't know what his birth family name was) that owned a miso factory, to marry the young daughter who had lost her father. He had been sent as a *yōshi*—an adopted son, through marriage—to carry on the Yamamoto lineage. (In accordance with a tradition practised in Japan, families without sons have the option of adopting a male acquaintance to keep title to the household under the family name.) However, when he arrived, the young widow decided to take him for herself. They had two sons. But one day, according to my mother, fed up with this life and having learned about adventures in the New World, Fukumatsu "kicked the miso bucket aside and walked to Yokohama, boarded a ship as a carpenter and came to Canada."

Several years later, while he was fishing in Steveston, British Columbia, his two sons arrived from Japan. Likely their mother had died. Fukumatsu put them to work and returned to Japan, where he soon remarried.

Interestingly, I was introduced a few years ago to a rare book titled 35 *Years of History of the Steveston Fishermen's Benevolent Society*. Originally published in Japan in 1935, the book records the struggles and conditions of the pioneer Japanese fishermen in Steveston. It was created as a legacy for the younger fishermen emigrating from Japan, by the hundreds at that time, to fish along the west coast of British Columbia and the Fraser River. The preface gives the names of men who took part in the society, and I was surprised and excited to see Fukumatsu Yamamoto, my grandfather, listed as a member in 1895.[1]

---

1   Teiji Kobayashi, ed., 35 *Years of History of the Steveston Fishermen's Benevolent Society*, 2013, Bill McNulty collection, Nikkei National Museum. English translation of Japanese text.

In her memoir, Mother recalls her own mother saying to her one day, while weaving cloth on a loom, "It is too bad that your father does not go to America anymore as other fathers are doing. You could have had the experience of wearing Western clothes instead of the ones I make for you."

There are many stories about Japanese emigrants from Wakayama Prefecture, particularly about those who came from Mio. One is about Kuno Gihei, who led the way, having come to Canada in about 1888 and then informed his home village about the abundance of fish in the Fraser River.

As a result, Mio was soon emptied of its men. My grandfathers from both sides of the family left for Canada soon after, holding "dreams of riches," but, I imagine, out of curiosity as well. Neither of them remained for long, and they left their sons in Canada to work. These men regularly sent remittances home, and it is said Mio-mura prospered and came to be known as "Amerika-mura" (America Village). Western living styles were emulated by its residents who drank coffee, wore Western clothes, adopted home furnishings such as chairs and introduced English words into their everyday language, pronounced in a new Japanese-English dialect.

Mother kept in close touch with her half-brothers throughout their lives here in Canada. Their sons, her nephews, were close to her age, one even a little older than she. I met one of them, Iwakazu Yamamoto, who lived in Steveston. He passed away a year before Mother did, and at his funeral I learned that he was one of the founding members of Steveston's early martial arts clubs.

I was surprised in reading Mother's memoir to learn she had been studying up until the time of her marriage, albeit traditional requirements, such as flower arrangement, tea ceremony, sewing and literature, toward becoming a proper wife. Of course, most likely this had to do with the fact that her father had prospered while in Canada and that, as tradition dictated, his two sons were sending remittances to him until they themselves married.

I had for many years carried a stereotypical image of Mother as a young girl working in the rice paddies with her parents. Perhaps that was because by the time I was old enough to ask about her background or listen to her stories, we had experienced such disruptions in our lives in Canada that her life in Japan had no relation to matters at hand. Our concerns then were only about survival.

Mother had, throughout it all, kept a diary, as many of her generation were doing; thus minute details, often easily forgotten, about specific events and names appear in her memoir. Father did not keep a diary, but he carefully filed his personal documents. Among these are the Imperial Japanese Government passport number 177683, dated the fifth month of the tenth year of the Taisho Era (that is, May 17, 1921). Another item is his third-class immigration identification card, documenting his departure via SS *Manila-Maru* from Yokohama, dated May 25, 1921—his first trip to Canada.

Born August 31, 1902, my father was the third son of Kichimatsu and Kinu Taguchi, of Mio, Wakayama Prefecture, Japan. He had two older brothers and a younger sister. As the third son, Torasaburo, along with his older brother, the second son, Konosuke, was sent in adulthood to two Nishikihama family relatives as *yōshi*. Accordingly, both my father and his brother, setting the last name Taguchi aside, became heads of two separate Nishikihama households, each inheriting both home and property. Nonetheless, Torasaburo came to Canada in 1921 under his birth surname, Taguchi. A certificate of filing notice of change of name in Victoria is dated April 7, 1927.

According to his passport, Torasaburo was nineteen years of age when he arrived in 1921. He had left Japan after finishing his education, eager to join his older brothers, who were already working as fishers on the west coast of British Columbia. However, upon arrival, he was told by his brothers to take a different path, that of learning for practical use the English language and Western customs, if he wished to remain in Canada.

He first served as a houseboy in Vancouver to pick up basic English, then began travelling across Canada by rail, perhaps working as a porter or a valet, living or stopping briefly in Moose Jaw, and then settled in Winnipeg. I recall a photo in our family album of him dressed in a white jacket, sitting with a couple of fellow employees in the dining room of the Canadian Pacific Railway's Royal Alexandra Hotel in Winnipeg. There was another photo of him with a couple of friends, seated in a convertible, smiling and wearing the period British wool tweed cap and knee-high socks over what looks like golf pants (which may have been the style of the time for young men). I read these images of Father as someone who was enjoying with his friends his bachelorhood in Canada.

I would learn from Father after our family moved to Winnipeg in 1950 that there had been Japanese immigrants living in Moose Jaw and in Winnipeg as early as the 1920s. One man Father met while he was living in Winnipeg was Mr. Harry Sasaki, who became a lifelong friend. (Older than Father, Mr. Sasaki was married to a white woman, which was unusual among Japanese immigrants of this time.) Another was Mr. Tachibana, who with his family operated a lampshade business. Father also knew the Nakauchis, whose daughter, Alice, later became an accomplished pianist.

When he was twenty-seven years of age and hadn't yet thought too seriously about his future, my father received an order from his parents to return home to Japan, where a bride had been arranged for him, a normal practice at the time. Among the documents saved by Father is a passport dated December 10, 1929, for both Torasaburo Taguchi and Sawae Taguchi. There is also a certificate of naturalization number 66565, which shows Father as a naturalized Canadian on the same date, under the name of Nishikihama.

Mother explains:

At the beginning of March 1929, under the government's new agreement with Japan that allowed entry to Canada of "picture brides," Nishikihama Torasaburo was allowed to return to his home in Mio with only a photograph of me to show, and to return to Canada with his bride.

After our marriage in Japan, we embarked on the *Empress of Canada* from Kobe, and I recall that since the emperor of Ethiopia was on this very ship, we were scheduled to arrive in Victoria sooner than usual [in seventeen days]. We suffered seasickness throughout the journey and couldn't lift our heads, never mind eat or drink. We finally arrived in

Victoria, when we learned that a stowaway had jumped and as a result searchlights were scanning the sea from the ship. The arrival time in Vancouver was delayed by one day, but on the following day, we reached the home of my brother-in-law, my husband's older brother Konosuke, in Steveston.

From that day forward, I began my life in Canada.

Konosuke-niisan's [*niisan* means "older brother"] home in Steveston was small but it was built on an acre and a half of land. The house was divided into two rooms, one a bedroom, the other a living room, with an extension to make another small bedroom and a kitchen. A further space was added for the *ofuro* [bathtub] and for a washroom.

There were six in their family, including four children, and soon after, in June, a fifth child was born. Then, in August, my sister-in-law's brother, Uyede Jitsuo, and his wife, Tsuyako, came from Skeena, and Tsuyako-san gave birth to her first baby. So I was busy washing diapers every morning.

My own first-born, a baby girl, Kikuko, arrived on November 20, 1931. But the joy was marred by the sad news subsequently from Japan that my father had died on December 25.

During the following year, my husband went to Skeena to help a friend fish for salmon. However, Canada was hit by a recession at this time. Even though my own family in Japan had little, I was raised supported by a household with Father and Mother together and remember my father always telling me how lucky I was that I was growing up without any worry about the price of rice. I had never in my past given such things a second thought. This was my first experience, in Canada.

At this time bread was five cents a loaf, a dozen eggs fifteen cents. Still, I searched for cheaper bread. People hired by farmers were working for twenty-five cents per hour, but even those jobs were scarce and they were open only to the regulars.

Grace's father, Torasaburo, came to Canada at the age of nineteen to join his brothers, who were working as fishers in Steveston. Later he became the buyer for the Codfish Cooperative Society, in the city of Vancouver. Author's personal collection

Family portrait taken in 1934. Grace sits on her father's lap, while her sister, Kikuko, stands in front of their mother. Author's personal collection

Salmon fishing was not good, and eventually I had to send my husband his fare to return home.

Two years later, I gave birth to my second daughter, Eiko.

We were still renting a space at my brother-in-law's home, and my husband went cod fishing when the salmon season ended.

At this time, *hakujin* [white], Japanese immigrant and Indigenous fishermen together established a Codfish Co-operative Sales Society. The fishermen brothers-in-law Taguchi Katsutaro and Nishikihama Konosuke were both members. My husband was hired for a buyer position by the society, so we moved to Vancouver during the following summer.

Our first address was at 522 Powell Street.

I wish I could find more information about the Codfish Co-operative Sales Society that Father had worked with. I have heard it was one of the earliest, if not the first, co-operative of this kind but so far have not been able to confirm that.

I recall as a child waving to Father as he left each morning for his workplace from the porch of my parents' second home at 510 Alexander Street, to which they had moved from 522 Powell Street with the birth of my brother Toyoaki. Father was always wearing a fedora and a three-piece suit, with a watch attached

Kikuko (left), Grace, and younger brother, Toyoaki, in 1937. Author's personal collection to a chain and fob tucked into his vest pocket, and often with spats over his shoes.

On weekend days, he would take my brother and me to the society's office at the docks, and I remember not only the loud squawks of the seagulls and the green water lapping under the wharf but also that we looked forward to being weighed on the fish scale. These are rare memories of joyful times spent with Father, as life was soon to change for all of us.

PAUERU GAI

Mother:

Vancouver was a very convenient place. On the 200 to 500 blocks of Powell and Alexander Streets, there was a variety of Japanese-owned stores. There were doctors, dentists and surgeons, and the gynecologist, Dr. Chikao Horii, was well known. His office was at 736 Granville Street. There were three or four fish markets, pharmacists, bathhouses and many restaurants. Fuji Chop Suey delivered food with just a phone call, and even a person like me from Japan who couldn't speak English had few daily issues.

In those days, not all houses and rental homes included a bath, just a toilet, so we regularly went to a public bath, of which there were many. Around that time, I can't remember if it was on Hastings or on Powell Street, there was a hairdresser named Watanabe-san who gave perms, so I used to go there. I remember that at the end of an electrical cord there was attached a pin around which hair was wrapped, and it seemed that with electricity, curl was achieved. There was a lot of gossiping at the hairdresser's.

My husband's two older brothers sent their wives back to Japan around this time, together with their children. The intention was that the children would receive a proper education. Katsutaro-niisan's [Father's oldest brother's] son, Taguchi Yoshiyo, who had learned the trade of chick sexing [separating male chicks from female ones] in Japan, came to Canada, depending on Nakamura Toru-san, an experienced chick sexer, of Strawberry Hill, and began working at Ōtsuki Yōkeijō [a chicken farm]. As a result, Katsutaro-niisan

Fuji Chop Suey, located at 314 Powell Street, was one of the many Japanese-owned businesses that made up the Paueru Gai neighbourhood. City of Vancouver Archives; Stuart Thomson photo. 99-3873

came into Vancouver every Monday to meet with his son, while Konosuke-niisan, living alone in Steveston, would also come to visit us on Mondays, saying he had some kind of meeting to attend.

In the meantime, my older daughter, Kikuko, started attending Sunday school. She was also registered in kin-

Powell United Church Kindergarten graduation class of 1939. Despite being raised Buddhists in Japan, Sawae and Torasaburo enrolled their children in the church-sponsored school. Author's personal collection

dergarten at the Japanese United Church [at the corner of Jackson Avenue and Powell Street, now the site of the Vancouver Buddhist Temple]. Subsequently, she was registered at Strathcona Elementary School and then at the Vancouver Japanese Language School on Alexander Street. We came to be on friendly terms with the Japanese language teachers, Tanaka Sensei and Motomochi Sensei.

My memories of this period, of course, are those of a child. The one-storey house on Alexander Street is no longer there today. A few steps led up to a small entrance porch. The porch opened into the main room, which served as both a living room and a dining room for entertaining guests. I remember hiding under the round table whenever guests came to the door. Beyond were two fairly large bedrooms, one used by my parents and my baby brother, Kenji, the other by my older sister, Kikuko, my younger brother, Toyoaki, and me. The kitchen where we had our daily family meals had a stove and an icebox, not yet a fridge.

Beyond the kitchen was a bathroom. I don't recall a bathtub, but this may be because we never used it. It would have been unfathomable in those days for any Japanese person to sit in a tub of water and wash. Japanese baths were about relaxing after one had, outside of the tub, washed oneself. We went with either Mother or Father to one of the public baths.

Where the back door would have been was a locked door instead. The main house had been extended backward—not upward, as additional spaces are usually constructed today—to add at least three apartment suites. Dr. Audrey Kobayashi, a professor in the Department of Geography and Planning at Queen's University in Kingston, Ontario, explained to me that this type of housing design, known in Japan as *nagaya* (a long house), was an efficient way of accommodating extra families on the same property.

Our home was located off Jackson Avenue, close to the Sailors' Rest Home and less than a block away from the Vancouver Japanese Language School. Across the street from us was Canco, the American Can Company. It had a large empty space, perhaps a parking lot, where many teenagers came to roller skate. I used to watch them with amazement, and Mother told me that as a preschool kid I imitated the skaters' motions, swinging my arms sideways to indicate the skates that I wanted her to buy for me. That never came to pass.

Another memory is watching schoolchildren walking by as they peeled and ate a piece of red ginger, dry and hot, covered with speckles of sugar. My mouth still waters when I think of it. Someone must have once given me a taste of it, as I longed for a piece, but Mother said it was not good for children. One day, however, I found some coins in a drawer in the kitchen and, gathering them, happily rushed along Powell Street to a Japanese-owned confectionery, of which there were many in those days. I asked for the ginger candy, but when the time came to pay and I offered the coins, the woman at the till looked at me, picked up the phone and called Mother. I was sent home in shame, though the woman did give me a couple of pieces of candy, not the ginger, to appease me. The coins, as it turned out, were not money but American tax tokens, and each silver piece had a hole in the middle. Likely Father, who in those days went to

Powell Street was the heart of Japantown, which hosted many parades and festivals. City of Vancouver Archives; Karl Haspel fonds. 300-136

Seattle a lot, had thrown them into the kitchen cabinet drawer.

Since our family was so connected with fishing, with my fisher uncles in Steveston and Father working at the Codfish Co-operative office, fish was our main diet. Returning to school after going home for lunch, I approached a friend from behind and put my hands over her eyes, saying "Guess who?" as we often used to do. She said it was easy to tell it was me because I smelled of fish!

Such were the trivialities of a childhood spent in Vancouver before 1942.

Today, fewer and fewer former residents remain who can tell stories about the neighbourhood where I grew up. Japantown is what the area became generally called in later years, by both Nisei and Sansei (second- and third-generation Japanese, respectively), who live without memory of the place. I recall this area being called Paueru Gai (Powell Street) by its Japanese immigrant residents, who had little or no English-language ability. My parents called it simply Paueru (Powell).

I believe names like Japantown (more often "Japtown") or Little Tokyo and even Chinatown are bestowed by outsiders (such as the media) to designate neighbourhoods occupied by those deemed "foreigners," not Canadians.

News about Japanese Canadian activities and events was in those days normally reported by local newspapers using derogatory language. For instance, even as the Vancouver Asahi baseball team became known as the most popular team in the 1920s into the '30s, team members were never talked about as Canadians in sports columns in the local newspapers. They were sometimes referred to as Japanese, more often called Japs or Nippons. It can be debated whether the word *Jap* was used as a derogatory term or as a short form (as one white author of a history book insisted in a conversation I had with him when I first met him at his book launch). However, the racist treatment of people of Japanese ancestry at this time would suggest, at least to me, that it was the former, a term used with disrespect.

One reason for the development of the Japanese settlement around Powell Street is that Hastings Mill, located at the foot of Dunlevy Avenue, hired Japanese and other Asian immigrants as they arrived in the late nineteenth century. The early workers, single men, lived on floating scows near the sawmill, while later arrivals lived in boarding or rooming houses run by Japanese entrepreneurs who began settling in this area. Early immigrants worked in all parts of the province in the logging, mining, fishing and canning industries and on railway construction. Many of these workers returned to Paueru Gai at the end of each contract for provisions and/or to wait for the next available work contract.

An agreement between Japan and Britain soon after the Anti-Asian riots of 1907, though curtailing immigration to Canada, allowed for Japanese wives to join their husbands. With the arrival of wives (many as "picture brides") and the subsequent arrival of children, Japanese immigrants began to settle more permanently in Canada, particularly on the west coast of British Columbia, wherever work was available.

"Picture bride" arrangements were an economic way of marriage between two strangers, and there are many stories of successful unions. However, oftentimes the photo sent to the potential bride did not reflect the true situation. Some men lied about their age or financial status to entice a woman to come from Japan. Even as they may have been disappointed upon arrival, most women, having no choice, stayed and assisted their husbands' new businesses or worked in canneries, often with babies tied onto their backs, to supplement the family's earnings. There were also cases of women rejecting marriage and—having nowhere else to go, since most came from poverty-stricken families in Japan and so were not able financially to return—ending up in prostitution, or even committing suicide. Such stories were told in *Tairiku Nippo*, the Japanese-language newspaper of the time, and later documented in book form by a Japanese writer, Miyoko Kudo, who once lived in Vancouver and researched immigrant lives.

By 1908, Paueru Gai was already turning into a self-sufficient infrastructure with businesses to sustain it. Some Japanese immigrant entrepreneurs even began to expand their operation bases, opening shops and businesses outside of Paueru Gai wherever mills were located and men were able to find employment, for example, Kitsilano and the North Shore. The success of Japanese immigrants was viewed with alarm by some, as indicated in a 1927 book, *Oriental Occupation of British Columbia*, by Tom MacInnes: "The Japanese and Chinese who are born and bred here, and educated by us, will control the mercantile of Vancouver as much as the Jews control the mercantile life of New York today."[2]

The growing Japanese immigrant population was noted in an article titled "One in Every 8 Babies Born in B.C. in 1931 Is Japanese" in the *Vancouver Province* (October 4, 1932). The article reported 1,342 Japanese babies registered in 1931, the year my older sister was born.

Ken Adachi, author of *The Enemy That Never Was: A History of Japanese Canadians*, says, "What the propagandists neglected to include in their perorations was the fact that the high rate of these menacing pregnancies could be only temporary. An unusual number of babies were being born simply because of the sudden influx of females of child-bearing age. ... By 1931, the high rate of child-bearing phase was patently over. ... Picture brides were no longer being freely admitted."[3]

---

2   Tom MacInnes, *Oriental Occupation of British Columbia* (Vancouver: Sun Publishing, 1927), quoted in Ken Adachi, *The Enemy That Never Was: A History of Japanese Canadians* (Toronto: McClelland & Stewart, 1976), 152.

3   Adachi, *The Enemy That Never Was*, 154.

The 1931 census shows British Columbia's population at 694,263. The Asian population was 50,951, which meant 1 in every 13 people was of Asian descent. There were 8,328 people of Japanese origin in Vancouver at that time, half of them residing in the Powell Street area.

Before 1942, the only political party in Canada that supported the right to franchise for all Canadians was the Co-operative Commonwealth Federation (the CCF, which later became the New Democratic Party). The earliest battle (1900–1903) was fought by an immigrant, the entrepreneur Tomekichi "Tomey" Homma, who, on behalf of Japanese Canadians and First Nations people barred from voting, took the province to court over the BC Provincial Elections Act. Although he won in the BC courts and at the Supreme Court of Canada, the Judicial Committee of the Privy Council in England, the final court of appeal at the time, confirmed the right of provinces to make the final decision—that is, to disqualify voters on the basis of race.

This was followed by the First World War Japanese Canadian soldiers winning the right to vote in 1931, after persistent efforts. In 1916, 222 Japanese Canadian volunteers had enlisted in the Canadian Expeditionary Force for military service overseas. However, the franchise was granted only for the lifetime of those soldiers who survived (53 were killed)—it was not extended to members of their family.

In May 1936, the Japanese Canadian Citizens League sent four Nisei delegates (Hideko Hyodo, a teacher; Minoru Kobayashi, an insurance agent; Edward Banno, a dentist; and S.J. Hayakawa, a university lecturer) to Ottawa's Special Committee on Elections and Franchise Acts of the House of Commons. While the special committee members' comments of surprise over the ease with which these delegates spoke English are recorded, the decision to grant the franchise was again deferred to the province of British Columbia, which had exclusive jurisdiction over civil rights.

Also to be remembered are the Nisei young men who, though interned with their families and friends in 1942, enlisted in Canada's military during the Second World War to show loyalty to their native country.

Finally, in 1948, Asian Canadians were granted the federal franchise, and Japanese Canadians cast their votes provincially for the first time in the 1949 election.

⁓⁂⁓

Though my parents were raised as Buddhists in Japan, they sent my sister and me to Rev. Kosaburo Shimizu's Japanese United Church Sunday School at the corner of Jackson Avenue and Powell Street. We also graduated from the church-sponsored kindergarten, taught in English by licensed white teachers. I believe, as young immigrant parents (Father having lived in Canada for more than ten years by then, and having mastered some English), they were preparing us for entry into the English-language public school system.

At the same time, my older sister and I were sent each day, after public school, to the Japanese Language School on Alexander Street. Japanese-language skills were necessary for young Japanese Canadians, with professional employment at this time possible only through Japanese businesses and companies. No matter their training or education, without the franchise, Japanese Canadians could not apply for licences to practice in professions here in Canada.

As children, my siblings and I spoke Japanese at home with our parents, and we were also in contact with relatives in Japan, in particular our grandmother, who regularly sent us gifts of books and games. I recall writing thank-you letters to her in Japanese.

On Powell Ground (now called Oppenheimer Park, since it was opened in 1902 by Vancouver's second mayor, David Oppenheimer, and later renamed in his honour), there were regular baseball practices and games. The Asahi baseball club (1914–1941) had various age levels of teams akin to a little league inviting boys under twelve to join. The Asahi team itself was the only non-white team to play in the local industrial leagues, and it was a source of community pride and joy (especially that baseball had already been introduced to Japan by the Americans, with Japanese players and teams visiting the United States and Canada as early as the 1920s). Developing a new strategy of baseball involving hard work, perseverance and good sportsmanship that came to be known later as "brain ball," the team, which had at first suffered unfair umpiring and booing fans, levelled the playing field, leading to fans cheering for them from both sides of the field.

The community arranged many other recreational activities and classes for both adults and their children, including martial arts, art and crafts, *odori* (Japanese dance) and music.

People living in Paueru Gai came from various prefectures in Japan, and they each had their own celebration events (some continuing even to this day). Everyone recognized each other through the different dialects they spoke. The Japanese Hall located in the Japanese Language School building hosted various public events, such as *shibai* or performances by locals, and concerts by guest artists or singers. I remember watching dubbed Japanese silent films there with my parents. The hall was the centre for community gatherings and for welcoming visitors from Japan, continuing cultural, social and political connections that were particularly important to immigrants who had not yet mastered the English language and also were not allowed to be full Canadian citizens.

For many years, I could not understand why Paueru Gai was viewed nostalgically among the surviving Issei (first-generation Japanese) as the good old days, since even cursory research reveals much to the contrary about their everyday lives as immigrants. The only answer I could come up with was that the early immigrants remembered the area as the centre of a support system. For those leaving behind a poverty-stricken Japan with great hopes, but finding in Canada that discrimination and unequal treatment were the norm, Paueru Gai became the new *furusato* (hometown), where immigrant families could live in relative peace. The hardships were endured as everyone strove to fulfill the dream of riches, some moving forward to acquiring homes, properties and businesses.

For the Nisei young adults, there was no such nostalgia—only daily disappointments and continuing hope for change. They had no opportunities for self-realization or the fulfillment of their dreams, even as their public school education emphasized the British concept of fair play. Born in Canada, with no lived knowledge of Japan, they believed themselves to be Canadians. But, denied the right to vote, they were excluded from taking full advantage of their education, even as many were graduating from university. As noted earlier, law, medicine, accounting, teaching and other professions requiring licensing to practise were available only to those with the franchise. It was understandable that some men, like my uncles, sent their children back to Japan to be educated, while they continued to work here in Canada.

My mother, a Japanese immigrant, recorded in her memoir only positive memories of living in Paueru Gai, the place where she and her husband began their married life with great dreams. Photographs in my parents' collection document each new addition to our family. Such photographs were taken not only to send the news to parents and grandparents in Japan, but also to show their family's well-being. Each new baby was entered in the family registry of Wakayama Prefecture.

OUTBREAK OF WAR

Mother:

In the fall of 1939, in compliance with my mother-in-law's request from Japan, I asked one of our friends who was going to Japan to take my older daughter, Kikuko, with them to visit with her grandmother. We had planned that the rest of the family would go to Japan the following year and bring her back with us. Unfortunately, we had not foreseen that the following year, due to Japan's war with China, we would have to cancel our plans.

Then, in December 1941, Japan attacked the American base in Hawaii. Vancouver's Japanese Language School was immediately closed, there were blackout practices in the city and we were restricted by curfew, not allowed to go out once the sun had set. Even if there was just a sliver of light leaking from a window, a patrolman came knocking at the door to give warnings. We had to cover the windows tightly with black sheets and only very carefully peek out to see what was going on.

Around this time, people of Chinese ancestry began wearing badges on their chests in order to not be mistaken for Japanese.

One early winter morning, Konosuke-niisan's brother-in-law, Uyede Jitsuo, of Skeena River, came to tell us that a Canadian soldier had come without any previous notice and told him and his friends to bring their fishing boats in to Vancouver. They had had no time for any preparation, and so he came knocking at our door to ask to borrow money so he might buy hot food for himself and for others who had come with him.

At about the same time, as people were bringing in their boats from the West Coast, we learned that one fisherman was missing. Everyone went searching for him along the coastal areas but they couldn't find him. Conjectures were rampant—something may have happened to the boat along the way, or he may have drifted to the American side and been mistaken for a Japanese spy. After several days had passed, a message came that he had been escorted home by a speedboat, and upon receiving permission from the RCMP through Morii Etsuji [a member of the subcommittee of Issei and Nisei formed during preparation for internment of Japanese Canadians to liaise with the RCMP], the family went to see him in a hospital. But he could not speak. His tongue had been cut, and when he asked for something to write with, no one had a pencil. The family regretted this forever.

He was likely the first Japanese Canadian victim of the Second World War here in Canada.

This was Oye Asako-san's husband. She and her husband had seven children, and the oldest, daughter Chiyoko, the only one married at that time, told me this story. Her husband, Sakai Kiyoshi, was a classmate of mine in elementary school in Mio, in Japan. During the postwar period [1945–1949], when we had moved to the Manitoba town of Whitemouth [before restrictions of movement were lifted], we became neighbours, and Asako-san visited me regularly and talked about this incident, still grieving.

People who were living in the Skeena River area or on Vancouver Island were held at Hastings Park Detention Centre before being moved to internment sites.

Since we were living in Vancouver, we were able to remain in our homes, but once a week we had to report to the RCMP office on Oak Street. We were required to register with the Government of Canada, and I remember that the officials spoke Japanese fluently. Naturalized Canadians like my husband and me were given pink registration cards to carry and Nisei were given white cards, each with a photo attached and on the back side a fingerprint, signature, address, occupation and vital statistics.

I recall on one occasion being asked by a United Church member which internment site we were being moved to. But I was expecting a child at the end of February or at the beginning of March, so my first concern at that time was looking for someone to take care of our home and family in my absence. So, when my brother-in-law Konosuke-niisan asked us to move from Vancouver to his home in Steveston next door to the Japanese Fishermen's Hospital, and told us to act quickly as transfers [moving trucks] would soon become scarce, we did so immediately without considering where we would eventually move to.

When I think about it now, in order to go anywhere, one would have to depart from Vancouver. But at that time, we did exactly as we were told by Konosuke-niisan and moved to Steveston. We moved there on February 28, and after taking care of our belongings in the new location, I gave birth to a daughter [Keiko] on March 1, at the Japanese Fishermen's Hospital.

I recall that for the first five or six months of my pregnancy, there had been many times when I had suffered a high fever through the night. From the day following the birth, I

Sawae's registration card, which she was required by law to carry with her at all times. Nikkei National Museum; 2002-10-9a

again had a high fever, and an arrangement was made with Dr. Kuwabara, who usually came to the hospital from morning to noon, to visit me. He placed a large bag of ice on my stomach. A couple of days later, my fever finally broke. The danger period had passed and I was able to return home in two weeks' time.

At that time, being young and naive, I didn't know that puerperal or childbed fever was a dangerous condition.

When I returned home, since I had gone into the hospital soon after moving into my brother-in-law's home, I found that nothing was in order. His friends were coming and going, and the wooden kitchen and living room floors were totally muddy. Today, the world is changed and it is quite normal for men to do some housework, but at that time it was expected that the woman should do it all. They should have discerned the condition I was in at that time, two weeks after birth, but they ignored this and I felt I had no option but to begin cleaning.

I felt the effects of this after we moved to the internment site a couple of months later. The veins in my hands swelled and my knees and shins hurt and gave me a lot of trouble. Somehow, in time, they healed naturally. But I felt a keen awareness of the importance of proper care after childbirth.

Every day we were hearing people talking about going to sugar beet farms or to government internment camps or to self-supporting sites, but I had just given birth and was busy nursing an infant.

Konosuke-niisan suggested that rather than going to a sugar beet farm, if we paid a rental fee, we could move in freedom. As I mentioned before, at that time, his wife and eight children were living away from him in Japan, so from the very beginning his plan had been for us to move with him. I was hearing that members of the United and Catholic churches were considering going to Greenwood or to Slocan or to another place together.

In the meantime, my older brother-in-law, Taguchi Katsutaro-niisan, whose family was also living in Japan, moved in with us and began taking his meals with us. During this time, my husband continued to work at the Codfish Co-operative and was commuting daily to Vancouver.

Japanese residences in Steveston, BC. With the outbreak of war, the family quickly relocated to uncle Konosuke's home in Steveston, where, the day after the move, Sawae gave birth to her third daughter, Keiko. Image E-03813 courtesy of the Royal BC Museum and Archives

Miyamoto Mantaro-san and Otsu Genji-san [both established Steveston fishermen], our good friends, often came to our place to discuss plans. They had decided to move to Minto Mines [an abandoned gold mining town in BC's Bridge River Valley], and so, in accordance with Konosuke-niisan's wishes, we also made the decision to go to Minto, a "self-supporting" internment site.

Katsutaro-niisan's son, Taguchi Yoshiyo, had already left home in mid-March or so to work at Manitoba's Hambley Hatchery as a chick sexer with Nakamura Toru-san. On their way to Manitoba, Nakamura-san, whose car licence required renewing, was stopped by the RCMP in Revelstoke, and the two of them were arrested and placed in a jail. But since the camera they carried had no suspicious photos in it, after a week they were freed. Since such things were happening, Katsutaro-niisan asked us to hold on to his old camera, together with his barber scissors, for safekeeping when he himself left for Manitoba. In any event, he couldn't cut his own hair so he had no need for the scissors, but they were useful for me, who had three male and two female heads of hair to cut in the family.

This camera moved with us during six or seven moves and settled at its last residence in Winnipeg. Since we had no interest in the camera and no time to use it during those years, we had forgotten that we had it. In time, one day I looked up on the shelf and wondered what it was that I had placed there, and in taking it down, I found it was the camera, the kind that you pull open to take pictures. It was the same kind that photographers used with a black cloth over it. I had heard that Katsutaro-niisan used to take and develop films at home.

The abrupt uprooting and removal of residents in 1942 is described in an article titled "The Life Blood Is Drained from the Heart of the Community" in the June 27, 1942, edition of the *New Canadian* (an English-language newspaper established by Nisei in 1938): "Powell Street was early adopted by the Japanese and under their care it just grew up. Now the Japanese are leaving and the street is beginning to look like a neglected orphan."

In her memoir, Mother recalls our family status and situation at the time Canada declared war with Japan. I was a child and now have little memory of this time except that we were moving. When I think back, there was a feeling of well-being and excitement as we packed to leave our home in Vancouver, as though we were going away on a holiday, this time to visit Uncle Konosuke in Steveston. Things important to a child are limited to the child's immediate needs and understanding. For instance, I recall to this day that on the last day of school, I proudly wore a red plaid pleated skirt and a pink puff-sleeved sweater, both made by Mother. I did not know that all Japanese Canadians, including some of my classmates, would soon be leaving, or for what reason. I do remember sadness in Mother's face, but I attributed it to her selling the new electric kitchen stove that she had so happily acquired recently.

I imagine it might be hard for the younger generations today to believe that our Canadian government had little or no conscience and acted in accordance with the urgings of racist politicians, particularly in BC. Of course, what happened to us cannot be blamed entirely on BC politicians or on the war with Japan; it was also a result of the racism and colonialism that allowed governments to believe it was their right to remove all people of Japanese origin from the West Coast. It bears remembering that the Second World War was also fought against Germany and Italy—but German and Italian Canadians were citizens, and we were not.

The fact that most people of Japanese ancestry living in Canada were naturalized Canadians (as my parents were) or born in Canada (as we children were) was meaningless. In the beginning, the removal was euphemistically called "evacuation" by the government, as though we were in need of protection.

At the same time, we were also deemed "security risks," and thus it was urgent we be removed from the hundred-mile West Coast security zone. This decision was made even as Prime Minister Mackenzie King was told by his own security forces (the RCMP and military advisers) that Japanese Canadians did not constitute a security risk so there was no need for such a removal. However, by invoking the War Measures Act, cabinet (not Parliament) was enabled to do this through orders-in-council. Labelled as "enemy aliens" (a term that should have been applied only to Japanese nationals, if at all), we were sent by order to government-prepared and -controlled internment sites beyond the security zone.

Our move to Steveston is not something I remember clearly. However, I have memories of running around my uncle's yard and his acre-and-a-half orchard with my brother Toyoaki, two and a half years younger than me, and a new friend, Masuo Yamashita, who was a few years older. Masuo's mother, known to us as Tonsa-ba (Aunt Tonsa), was not a relation but an old friend from the same prefecture in Japan who looked after us and our younger brother, Kenji, not yet three at that time, while Mother was in the hospital. I remember us standing by the fence that separated our uncle's property from the Japanese Fishermen's Hospital, waving to our mother, who waved back from the hospital window.

After Mother returned home from the hospital with our baby sister, Keiko, and while Father was commuting daily to Vancouver to his job, Uncle Konosuke was meeting with his friends, making the decision as to which internment site we should move to.

I recall Mother having several wooden boxes made to pack the treasures she would be leaving behind: dishes (Japanese porcelain sets for each season), books, ornaments such as Boys' and Girls' Festival dolls, kimonos she had brought from Japan, all things that were precious to save and so had been brought here to Steveston from Vancouver but were not necessary to take with us, for we expected to be away only for the duration of the war. She placed the boxes in the storage shed behind my uncle's house, padlocking the door.

She was never to see her treasures again. Homes were vandalized and objects stolen soon after we had moved to the internment site, with many items appearing at auctions, we were later told.

Minto Mines

Mother:

We took with us rice, as much as we could carry, canned foods, other groceries, tea and a minimum number of dishes, pots and pans and left in early April 1942, forty days after my giving birth, taking a Union Steamship Company boat from where the Bayshore Inn is located today in Vancouver and arriving in Squamish some four hours later.

Seeing Squamish for the first time, I was impressed by the astonishing beauty of the soaring cliffs that I had never seen even in pictures, the vividness of the colours and the mysteriousness of the granite face of the mountains. I felt as if I were in a hallucinatory dream.

We then took a train that chugged through the valleys and along a river for a hundred miles or more, and I remember arriving after six hours at Bridge River, late at night. A friend, Nishihama Naokichi-san, who had earlier gone to Bridge River, welcomed us, bringing us tea. We spent the night on the coach train, and then a truck came for us early the next morning. We sat with the children, me carrying the newborn baby, on a long wooden bench on the back of the truck and were then driven up the high Mission Mountain on curved roads for about two hours until we came to the peak. My ears popped, so it must have been high altitude.

Some people who had come earlier were living in the hotel in Minto, and Takeuchi Chisato-san, of Union Fish in Vancouver, helped us to locate on the second floor above the grocery store next to the hotel. Fortunately, there was hot water, but since we had children, we said we needed a house,

Postcard showing Minto City and the surrounding mountains. Simon Fraser University Library; MSC130-1891-01

and so we moved into one the next day. But this house was too small even with just our family, and since my husband's brother was to live with us, a larger house was found a distance away and pulled into the townsite. An additional room was added, together with a *furoba* [bathroom]. There was an outdoor storage house. A side-by-side toilet shack was built to service our home and the one next door. Picking wood from the forest, we made a fire in the kitchen stove.

Konosuke-niisan's daily routine was to listen to the shortwave radio at the hotel and to write down the daily news from Japan to share with his friends.

In front of the house, we planted potatoes and various other vegetables. The men dug a hole under the house so we could store the rice we had brought and the potatoes and vegetables we would soon be harvesting, together with other groceries.

We learned that during the mining era, our house had been used by a miner family. Since the outside walls were only tarpapered, during the winter snow blew in through the cracks. It was a cold and drafty house. Otsu Genji-san and his brother-in-law, Miyamoto Mantaro-san, and their families lived in a large house a distance away. I was told that their house had been a brothel at the peak of the gold rush. Kagetsu Eikichi-san and Hide-san's house was also a distance away. So whenever members of these families came to shop, they had to pass through our back lane.

The family names of our neighbours were Furukawa, Watada and Yoneda to the right and, to the immediate left, Nishi no Obasan [*obasan* means "aunt" or "older woman"] living with her adult son and daughter, Toshinami and Namiko. And next, the Murakami family.

Every morning Minto's mayor, Mr. Bill Davidson, would mount his horse and, together with several other horses wearing bells around their necks sounding *chirin, chirin*, ride to a destination in the mountain area and return at night. He was observed to be looking at the high mountains with binoculars and, upon discovering prey, would shoot at it, causing a loud echoing sound in the village. If his target was hit, he took four or five hunting dogs to retrieve the prey.

As soon as vegetables, for instance, the peas, began sprouting, deer families would come to eat both the sprouts and their roots. Even with a six-foot-high fence around the garden, they would leap over, and sometimes when we discovered them in the garden, they would stop and look at us, much to the children's delight and pleasure, and would not run off until we yelled at them.

Soon, a school was established in the reactivated ghost town of Minto, and former teachers like Ms. Kazu Umemoto, as well as Mr. George Tamaki, a university graduate, were designated to teach.

In my family, our second daughter, Eiko, and first son, Toyoaki, began attending school. One day during the summertime, it was announced a field day event would take place a little distance away, so I took my four children and went to watch. Children's races, tug-of-war and all sorts of games were played, and then there were races for the parents. In my childhood I had won prizes on field days, so I had confidence in my athletic abilities, but it was of no use; now, as a mother of five children, my legs would not live up to my expectations!

Opposite our house at the base of the low mountain, there was a shrine with a *torii*, a Japanese Shinto temple gate that Morii Etsuji-san had built. In the evenings, Shoji Eitaro-san played the *shakuhachi* [bamboo flute] and the quiet melody resonated throughout Minto. These were truly peaceful moments.

To supplement our winter fuel, my six-year-old son would tag along with his uncle to the mountainside and bring back dry wood, together with the village gossip, for instance, where sake was being made and who was making miso. Next door to me was the elderly woman Nishi-san, who was renowned in Steveston for her miso and *kōji* [malted rice], while others in the village were experts in making sake, miso, tofu and even shoyu [soy sauce].

At that time in Minto there were men who obtained sawmill work in nearby Devine. A friend, Sakata Tomi-san, came from Bridge River to work there and stayed with us. Acting on Konosuke-niisan's idea, my husband ordered some salmon from Vancouver, cleaned them in our storage shack and shared them with our friends and neighbours.

The first winter was a very cold one. One night there was a fire, and our men all rushed over to help douse it. It was at Mayor Davidson's house. When the men returned, I remember, there were icicles hanging from their eyebrows and noses. After a couple of cold days, the water pipes near our home froze and burst, and all night long the water was left to flow and freeze to become a splendid ice sculpture. The winter of 1942, from stories I have heard since, seemed to have been the coldest of winters everywhere. I continue to regret that the ice sculpture was not photographed with the forgotten camera.

Snow fell on Minto's mountains and young people enjoyed skiing.

In this way, the harsh and nightmarish year ended.

As usual, when evening came, sounds of Mr. Shoji's shakuhachi came from the mountainside, and the noisy flow of the Fraser River echoed in the valley. In the harsh embrace of Mother Nature, where there was no danger of being expelled, we felt thankful that at least we were surviving, supported by friends.

One day in 1944, the Red Cross, through Maruyama Tsurukichi-san, sent miso, shoyu and tea as comfort gifts to all persons of Japanese ancestry residing in foreign countries. I was told to bring a container and I gratefully accepted the gift. It was a gift from Japan, which was itself suffering from famine.

Our youngest daughter, less than a year old, began walking. Every evening after dinner during the summertime, together with Sakata-san from Bridge River, the family all sat outside to enjoy conversing in the cool evening breeze.

Niisan began at this time to lift Keiko by holding her head between his hands, saying "*Takai, takai* [up, up],"and while usually the child would hold on to his hands, one day when he lifted her, I felt that he was treating her head like a chicken's neck. I repressed my concerns and pretended that I didn't see, but the next day he did the same thing. To someone who is a father of eight children, I could not restrain myself any longer and confronted him angrily: "Niisan, what are you doing? If this child becomes crippled, are you going to take responsibility for her?"

After a while, with the end of the war not easily foreseen, Niisan, with help from a friend, Nishihama Naokichi-san, left Minto to move to a farm in Vernon. I felt it was likely due to his taking offence at my remarks. It was around April 1944.

At about this time, Keiko caught a cold and her fever would not subside. We bought some medicine from Nimisan; however, she didn't improve. We called a doctor in Bralorne for a prognosis. Even though the medicine given to

Minto City, established as a mining townsite in 1934, was converted into a self-supporting internment site in 1942, after the closure of the mine. University of British Columbia; Uno Langmann Family Collection of British Columbia Photographs. UL_1645_0008

us was only children's Aspirin, when it was administered the fever rose sharply and she appeared to be in distress.

Nishi no Obasan from next door came in and said, "You go and eat. I will look after her." She substituted for me, fanning the child. I could hear her say, "Poor child, I feel sorry for you."

I wondered, in my ignorance, if the fever was not due to the children's Aspirin, and whether withdrawing the medicine was the right answer or not. However, she gradually recovered. Unlike today, I had no such things as vitamins or supplements, and I was forced to make these decisions on my own whenever there was illness in the family.

Minto was one of five locations in the Bridge River–Lillooet area used as Japanese Canadian self-supporting internment sites. I was not aware of what this meant until recently. The fact is that the arrangement was made by the wealthy, for the wealthy, supported by the British Columbia Security Commission.

East Lillooet was one of the five self-supporting internment sites in the Bridge River area; over 1,000 internees left their West Coast homes for these camps. Nikkei National Museum; Genzaburo and Kimiko Nakamura Family collection. 2002-10-9a

Though wealthy families were uprooted from their homes along with some 22,000 others living on the west coast of British Columbia, a special consideration was made available to those willing to pay for transportation and rent. Self-supporting sites were established in Lillooet, Bridge River, Minto, McGillivray Falls and Christina Lake, and 1,161 internees paid the government's expenses for their own uprooting. There is no doubt that all internees in the end paid for the cost of their uprooting, considering the forced sale of homes, businesses and personal property, left behind in trust, to the Custodian of Enemy Property. However, wealthy families had the option of choosing one of these sites. Thus, even though they were forced to leave their West Coast homes and businesses, through their ability to pay both rent and transportation costs, they were given the option to live in relative comfort, as, I recall, many families in Minto did.

Unlike those sent to government-prepared camp sites, where often two families were assigned to live in each of the barrack-like shacks the government had prepared, with each family member allowed to bring only one suitcase of necessities (leaving all personal properties behind), most who moved to the self-supporting site of Minto brought with them all their personal belongings, including home furnishings. Their homes in Minto were largely houses recently vacated by middle-class miner families, and the homes were of various sizes, with fenced-in yards, on established streets.

Mother used to say the reason we ended up in Minto had nothing to do with wealth but with following Father's older brother's request to go with him and his established Steveston fisher family friends. As Mother's memoir indicates, she and my father were certainly not in a position where they could have afforded to go to a self-supporting site such as Minto on their own.

Some who settled in such self-supporting areas may have had a political agenda in choosing such sites. Many younger men living in hardship and experiencing economic difficulties, including Father, soon found work in a nearby mill. In this way, they were able to pay rent and maintain their households.

As children, our thoughts did not dwell on affordability or on the always lingering worry, particularly among the Issei, over who would win the war, which might determine what would happen to us next. We just enjoyed each day, playing with our newfound friends in the beautiful open valley, made comfortable by the gardens of flowers and vegetables planted by our parents, and enclosed by huge mountain ranges, with the sound of the rapids not too far away—Gun Creek, beside which community and school class picnics were often held.

While at least one incident prevents me from looking back on my life in Minto as entirely happy, as I read Mother's account, some pleasant memories appeared in my mind. I could see Mother wearing a large straw hat, under which a white *tenugui* (a light, rectangular Japanese towel) was wrapped around her long hair, which was the style of most women her age at that time. She wore a white Japanese-style apron with sleeves, laced at the back, as did most of the other mothers as they worked the vegetable gardens, weeding with hoes while chatting and sharing stories.

Under different circumstances, this scene could be interpreted as idyllic. We were surrounded by beautiful mountains and trees. As Mother writes, the vegetable gardens, beautifully appointed and designed with flowers blooming along the borders, were visited by deer families, especially in the early morning hours. Gardens were allocated to each family and took up the large empty spaces between homes not far from the town centre. The garden areas were surrounded by fences made of newly peeled logs. These had been built by the new residents soon after they settled in this former gold mining town.

Vegetables of all kinds, used for both Japanese and Western-style cooking, were grown to maintain each family throughout the year. I wonder today if some families had brought seeds, as many of the vegetables were of Japanese origin, such as *kyūri* (Japanese cucumber), *nappa* (cabbage), *daikon* (Japanese radish), *kabocha* (squash), various *mame* (peas and beans, for example, *sayaendō*, *edamame* and *soramame*) and herbs such as *shiso* (purple mint).

When my baby sister, Keiko, was ill, I recall that Mother always had beside her not only a thermometer for checking body temperature but also a Japanese medical book, very thick (about three to four inches), with a wine leather or leather-like cover. I used to see her consulting the book whenever any of us was ill. When my sister had the high fever, though Mother doesn't mention it in her memoir, I remember her going out into the garden and digging up some earthworms, which she chopped and minced to make a poultice that she wrapped around the soles of my sister's feet. How effective this was I don't know, as I never tried it with my own sons, but the remedy likely came out of her medical book.

Mother had her own family health-care rules. We children were taught to gargle with warm salt water every night before going to bed, after brushing our teeth with salt. I hated the smelly mustard plaster she placed on my chest when, during the hot summer months, I invariably came down with the flu.

I remember also that Mother went to see Etsuji Morii, known to have direct access to the RCMP, to request medical help for baby Keiko. There was no doctor in town so one had to be accessed from a neighbouring town, Bralorne. In order to do this, RCMP permission was required.

I distinctly remember Mother placing money in an envelope when she went to request such help. She also took money in an envelope to pray at the *odaisan*, the beautiful Shinto wooden shrine with the *torii* gate, which Etsuji Morii had built behind his home on the mountainside. I wonder now who kept the proceeds, or how such money was used, as certainly Mother was not the only one who did this. It was Japanese custom to make such offerings when praying at a shrine or a temple. Etsuji Morii was referred to as "the godfather" by some members of our community, since he had owned a private gambling den in Vancouver before the war, supported, we heard, by the local police.

Mother depended on and consulted Mrs. Miwa, a registered nurse living with her family not far from us. I remember visiting the Miwa family, which was quite different from mine, as the parents were Nisei and spoke English. Particularly, I remember reading comic books for the first time while visiting with their daughter Tama and her siblings. Tama was a classmate. Many years later, I was to meet her again, along with her beautiful and talented pianist daughter, Alison Nishihara, in Vancouver.

Once, when I had to visit the dentist, I was taken to Bralorne in a taxi, called a "stage" by the locals, driven by Toragoro Nimi. Mr. Nimi was an entrepreneur who had operated a pharmacy in Vancouver before the war. His son, Bobby, as I called him, was my classmate here in Minto and had earlier graduated from Vancouver Japanese United Church kindergarten with me. When my baby sister was ill, it was to Mr. Nimi that my mother went to buy the Aspirins to reduce Keiko's fever.

In Minto, there was, as I recall, a grocery store, a hotel, an apartment building and a post office in the main street area. Minto's grocery store carried everything and we lacked for nothing, except perhaps some ingredients required for a proper Japanese meal. Bread and various sweets were baked daily and sold there. I remember that on certain evenings, after I had played Chinese checkers with my uncle and lost to him, to soothe my hurt feelings he would offer me money so I could run over to the grocery store and pick up a cake, a rare treat in those days (though Mother soon learned to bake both cake and bread).

There are many kind and wonderful people in my memories of Minto. The teachers Mr. Tamaki, Mrs. Umemoto and Ms. Amy Uchida, and her sister Ms. Chizu Uchida, are names that come to mind easily.

Classes were taught by our own community's educated people, directed by the provincial curriculum. Classmates Yohko Noda, Emiko Furukawa, Tama Miwa and Yoko Uyede were some of my best friends.

I remember some fathers and sons making large wooden cages in which they would place a squirrel. The poor squirrel scrambled up and down a makeshift tree inside.

I also remember pleading with Mother to ask another mother if her son, Tadashi, one of my classmates, would carve me a wooden brooch like the one I saw his sister, Sumire, wearing and that I envied. It was in the shape of a Scottie dog with the word *Minto* printed on it. He agreed. I wish I had taken better care of that brooch, as sometime during our many moves I lost it. But there is at least one photo remaining of me wearing it.

My brother Toyoaki spent a lot of his time with his friends at Mayor Davidson's ranch, watching the many horses the mayor kept, at times even watching them being bred. As boys, they were allowed a lot of freedom to explore the area. Being a girl and an older sister, I spent most of my spare time helping Mother with household chores, as well as babysitting. More often than not, my baby sister was tied to my back in the traditional manner. Of course, in those days we had neither strollers nor baby carriages, at least not in my family, though as I recall there were a few young boys riding bicycles, one delivering newspapers.

Of much consequence, though I did not appreciate it at the time, was that Mother continued the Japanese-language lessons I had already started when we left Vancouver for Minto. Each day, after returning home from public school and eating the *oyatsu* (a little snack, say, an apple) left for me on the kitchen table, I was required to sit down and study from my Japanese-language textbook for an hour under her direction. I resented being forced to sit daily, after being at school all day, to attend her school while my friends and my brothers were outdoors playing.

Mother had gathered textbooks from friends whose children had finished a level or had given up studying Japanese (as most had) when they moved to the various internment sites. I would read out loud, learn to write a new *kanji* (Chinese/Japanese character) or take my weekly tests while she did the daily washing in the adjoining *furoba* with the door ajar. She yelled out directions to jog my memory when there was a recently learned kanji I had already forgotten, offering me hints, for example, the kanji radical or its constituent parts.

I learned that the Japanese kanji for the *ei* of my name, Eiko (the ending *-ko* meaning "child"), identified me as an "English" child, born to naturalized Canadians here in Canada, a British colony. My older sister, on the other hand, being the first-born child of Japanese immigrants, was named Kikuko, the *kiku*, or "chrysanthemum," signifying the imperial crest of Japan.

Years later, in studying classical Japanese at the University of British Columbia as an additional language requirement for a graduate studies program in Asian art history, I realized how lucky I was that she had had the foresight to teach me the basics. She had taught me so well that I was able, at least to some extent, to recognize meanings held within the kanji structure and to move forward. After retirement from my professional career, I continued to improve my Japanese enough that when I was invited to teach visiting Japanese students a course in Japanese-to-English translation, I decided to try it and in fact enjoyed it.

Perhaps one reason Mother felt the necessity to teach me proper Japanese was that in Minto there were many fisher families from Steveston, friends of my uncle Konosuke. Most came from Wakayama Prefecture, largely from the village of Mio, and spoke mainly the Kansai (or Osaka-area) dialect. This dialect was quite different from the Kanto dialect of the Tokyo area, which was snobbishly considered to be standard formal Japanese at that time. The Kansai dialect was often mangled, spoken crudely (like slang) among fishermen and picked up by their children. I thought it was grown-up and sophisticated, but when I tried it at home, Mother roundly scolded me, saying this was *ryōshi no kotoba* (fishermen's language), not fit for girls to use. My mother's language school continued for the next five years or so, giving me a solid foundation upon which to build.

Another benefit of her teaching was that through the years following internment, when we had settled into the larger society, I was useful as Mother's interpreter. Wherever she went, to the grocery store, to the doctor's office, to schools to meet with my younger brothers' teachers, I was always there, since Father was usually working away from us. When she and Father later moved back to the West Coast from Winnipeg, where we'd all been living, I was able to write to her in Japanese. As well, when any urgency arose, we had phone discussions in Japanese. These were things most Japanese Canadians my age, including my brothers, were not able to do. They had lost the language of their parents almost entirely, and so communication in pidgin English became the norm in conversations with parents.

My best memories of family life in Minto are the evenings we spent after bath. Uncle Konosuke had brought from Steveston his *ofuro* (Japanese-style wooden bathtub). He could not part with it, so he had paid for the transportation cost from Steveston to Minto. He had an additional room built at the back of our house and installed the tub, to our great daily comfort.

My parents, having sold their furnishings when we moved from Vancouver to Steveston, had brought to Minto only the bare necessities. Any family treasures were, as mentioned, packed in boxes and locked in the storage shed behind Uncle's home in Steveston. The only large pieces we had brought to Minto were Mother's sewing machine, which we were not allowed to touch (it represented for her the only source of dignity in our lives at that time), and a large trunk Father had bought at T. Eaton & Company in Winnipeg during his bachelor days. The trunk travelled with us to Minto, filled not only with clothes, *futon* (bedding) and various household necessities but also with books Mother could not part with and, fortunately, family photo albums, something many families lost. The trunk remains with me to this day.

The Nishi family members next door came most evenings to bathe in our *furo*, or *ofuro*, as we called it, with the honorific o added to an object or person. Nishi no Obasan was related to us through marriage. Her first daughter, Fujiko-san, was married to my father's relative, To-motaro Tsuchiya. My parents called him Tomo-yan (*yan* being like *san*, but a more personal and affectionate term), while we children called him Tomoyan-ojisan (Uncle Tomo-yan).

(Mr. and Mrs. Tsuchiya had gone directly to Manitoba in 1942. They were living on a farm in Brunkild, and we had heard they were generously accepted, likened to family members, by a family named Hoffman. Later on, when I was about twelve and we had moved to Manitoba, I remember Mr. and Mrs. Tsuchiya visiting us once and my returning with them to Brunkild for a week or so. I did not know then, but have since learned, that before the war, I had been promised to them for adoption since they had no children and I was my parents' second daughter. But Mother, already parted from her first daughter, could not release me. I remember enjoying this visit and meeting the Hoffman family, who had a daughter about my age. Tomoyan-ojisan was very artistic and also a skilled carpenter. He built a silo on the Hoffman farm and, I am told, later a home for the Hoffman son when he married. During my brief visit, Tomoyan-ojisan spent a couple of evenings with me cutting up a large Eaton's cardboard box into small cards, then painting pictures and writing calligraphic verse on each to produce a set of a Japanese card game popular with adults in those days. He then taught me to play. This beautiful handmade set of cards, like my Scottie brooch made by Tadashi Sakamoto, was lost during our family's several moves. Things of importance to children got lost easily in those days, as we packed to move from one place to another.)

The *furoba* was where my mother did the daily washing on the scrub board. As she hung out the clothes to dry on a line that extended from our front porch to a tall pine tree, I could sometime hear her responding to the robin that came to perch on the same pine branch each morning: "Minto, minto, chirrrp."

The *ofuro* was installed with a platform built above floor level attached alongside it. Inside the tub was a tubular stove, fed from the outside with wood. Mother tended it, ensuring the water remained at a comfortable temperature. We would sit on little stools placed on the platform outside the tub to wash and rinse ourselves before entering the tub to relax. Inside the square tub were benches, one on each side, where we would sit to soak in the clear, warm water.

Usually Father, coming home from his sawmill work nearby, was given the first turn with his brother, Konosuke. They would sit and relax in the tub, catching up on the day's events. Next were the children, helped by Mother. She would bathe last, after everyone else (including

The family in Minto City before preparing to relocate to Manitoba in 1945 following the Canadian government's dispersal policy, which forced the expulsion of Japanese Canadians from the West Coast. Author's personal collection

our neighbour, Nishi no Obasan, who came weekly) had bathed, and then clean out the tub before going to bed.

As children we looked forward to Nishi no Obasan entering our back door, at times saying, "Did you notice? I think someone died last night. I saw a *tamashii* [a spirit] flying. Did you see it?"

Of course, no one had, but we children, now in our *nemaki* (Japanese-style nightshirt), would wait for her to finish bathing, knowing there was a story to follow. It was usually a Japanese ghost story that kept us awake longer than my mother would have wished.

While we sat totally rapt in Obasan's stories, Mother would be taking her baking out of the oven—bread and often *anpan* (buns with a sweet bean filling), which she had learned to bake from Namiko Nishi, daughter of Nishi no Obasan. Nami-chan (*chan* is another term of affection, as opposed to the more formal *san*), who was single and perhaps in her mid-twenties, made our birthday cakes and cookies for us.

Mother would also heat up some *amazake* (sweet rice wine), which she had learned to make from Nishi no Obasan, for the adults. Supervised by elders like Nishi no Obasan, mothers in Minto would gather together to help one another make not only rice wine (though this recipe was usually kept secret) but also the miso, tofu and shoyu required for proper Japanese cooking.

As children of immigrant, now interned, parents, we were not in the habit of receiving Christmas gifts, certainly not the sort my grandchildren receive today. The New Year's celebration was traditionally more special. But my parents always made sure there was a gift for each of us. There was no tree, no decorations, but stockings were hung near the beds, in which we would find in the morning some nuts to crack and usually an orange, perhaps continuing a custom followed before the war when we used to get oranges from Japan.

Usually, the Christmas present each of us received was not a surprise, since it was something that we had been requesting of our parents. I recall going with Mother to Woodward's department store in Vancouver once to buy me a Western doll for a Christmas present. (My grandmother had already sent me a Japanese doll dressed in a kimono.) I was thrilled that the doll opened and closed her eyes and wore a plaid skirt (much like the one Mother had made for me) and a tam-o'-shanter over her auburn hair.

There were no expensive gifts in Minto, only small items my parents managed to order from the Eaton's mail-order catalogue. My gift was usually a book, and when I was about ten, I was given Charlotte Brontë's *Jane Eyre*, a nineteenth-century novel that was thought to address, among other things, early women's issues. I think the book was chosen because it had a girl's name in the title, not for its content, which my parents would have had no idea about. I think Mother remembered that when I was in grade two I used to borrow Elsie Dinsmore series books from the Carnegie Library in Vancouver. *Jane Eyre* was not an appropriate book for a ten-year-old, but when the female teachers and older students saw me with it, they asked to borrow it. I remember feeling proud of Mother for having chosen this book for me.

Unfortunately, among such childhood memories of being well cared for by parents, neighbours and our new community, there is a negative memory too. On one evening trip to the grocery store to buy a cake, a treat offered by my uncle, I was walked partway home by a young man, perhaps in his late twenties, who struck up a friendly conversation with me. Unlike today, when children are taught not to speak to or go near strangers, in Minto we had no fear of strangers. We were all members of this community, an extended family.

I was about eleven years old at that time and knew nothing about the birds and the bees. So I did not fully comprehend what happened when he grabbed me and kissed me fully on the mouth. I had seen some Western comic strip images and movie ads where such things occurred between a man and a woman. But I had never seen Japanese adults (not even parents) publicly show such affection. Such conduct was certainly not part of Japanese custom or culture.

It was not a pleasant experience. Even as the young man told me he liked me and wanted to be friends, I did not have a comfortable or happy feeling about his actions. I went home, holding the cake, and stood for a while on the front steps, fidgeting, not knowing what to do. When Mother opened the door and called out "What are you doing? We're waiting for you!" I entered and never said a word about what had passed.

I was too young and inexperienced to put two and two together and certainly to worry about whether this had happened to any other girl in Minto. The fact that I did not tell anyone about the incident, however, spoke volumes. Obviously, I knew that something improper had happened. I actually told no one about this until recently, when I renewed a friendship in Vancouver with Bobby, my kindergarten classmate, also a schoolmate in Minto. Bob remembered the young man's family name. I wonder today if this young man was just experimenting or was practising something with me that he did not have the nerve (or chance) to do with a young woman in Minto, especially considering our culture. I would like to think this, rather than believe otherwise.

I avoided the young man from then on, but the avoidance made my life in Minto a bit difficult. I was filled with anxieties, and I did not even realize until recently that I had avoided talking about Minto since leaving in 1945. That changed after I read Mother's memoir and saw that, even though she and Father were daily struggling to deal with their drastically changed lives, their hopes and dreams completely shattered, she still found some light moments from Minto to remember and to write about.

DISPERSAL

Mother:

Around this time [March 1945], the government proclaimed a dispersal policy by which we had to make a decision to go either to points east of the Rockies or to Japan. It was said to be a loyalty test.

Two hundred dollars in cash and travel fare were offered by the government to those who chose to go to Japan, and they would have to register their intent. [Individuals could take only 150 pounds of personal effects.] The first group was scheduled to leave on May 22, 1946. Because we had an elderly mother and a daughter in Japan, we signed on, but with the evident losses of war and the poor conditions in Japan, we pondered the best thing to do and ended up withdrawing our application.

We then decided to go to Manitoba, where Katsutaro-niisan was living. Another reason for this choice was that my husband had lived in Manitoba, in Winnipeg, at one time in his past, before we were married, and was familiar with the city.

Everyone living in Minto, Greenwood, Tashme and Revelstoke was making a decision individually within the limited framework of the time and places offered.

Under supervision of the RCMP, with four children, the oldest now eleven, we left Minto behind. We arrived in Lillooet on the first night of travel and were refused a hotel room. Another hotel accepted us. I thought it was not much wonder that we were refused, with four children! That evening, a friend came to meet with us and we talked until mid-

A crowded train station at Greenwood, BC. After the war, Japanese residents of the internment sites, including those at Greenwood, were forced to choose between moving East of the Rockies or deportation to Japan. Nikkei National Museum; Tasaka Family Collection. 2011-83-1-33

night. The following morning, continuing the train travel, we stopped at Vernon, where Konosuke-niisan was living on an orchard farm. I was not aware that there had been a letter from this brother to my husband.

The town of Vernon was full of Canadian soldiers, whether at the station or in the hotel. I met a friend from the past near the station. In contrast to the solitary quiet of Minto, coming to a place like this we became more aware of the fact of wartime. In the high hills of Vernon there were sounds of soldiers training, shooting and firing. We went to Mr. Chiba's farm, where my husband's brother was living and working.

We had arrived at lunchtime and were invited to eat with them. It was cherry season and the trees were full of cherries, a colourful sight to behold. Our two sons, Toyoaki and Kenji, receiving permission, climbed up a tree and ate the cherries.

My husband and his brother went into a room to talk, while the children and I waited in the garden. I pretty well knew what they were talking about, likely money matters.

A train carrying Japanese Canadians uprooted from their homes in Vancouver stopped in the Slocan Valley, circa 1942. Photographer: Leonard Frank. Nikkei National Museum; Alex Eastwood collection. 1994.69.4.29

But I did wonder if it was about the accounting for the salmon ordered from the Vancouver fish market, or about the board my brother-in-law didn't pay and the rent we paid when he lived with us. But then I thought he should have settled this before leaving Minto. I suspected I was excluded from their discussion now because he was still bothered by what I had said to him when he lived with us about lifting baby Keiko by the head. In order for someone outside of the immediate family to live together, there needs to be a mutual feeling of respect and consideration.

They came out of their meeting without any explanation. We went and had dinner at the Chinese restaurant near the station and then left for Manitoba, our family of six boarding the train, leaving Niisan in Vernon.

Whenever we boarded any moving vehicle, Eiko and I suffered motion sickness, so we always carried a large jam tin. But Kenji, the younger son, who had climbed a tree and eaten cherries during the afternoon, had an upset stomach and ran to the train washroom but didn't quite make it in time. Everything came out, and he had to be changed completely. Such were the highlights of our journey, but after two nights we arrived safely in Winnipeg, just before noon.

Arriving at this eastern point, I thought we would have more freedom. However, due to continued restrictions, the RCMP and the Security Commission representatives were there to meet us, and we were taken outside of Winnipeg to a vegetable farm in Middlechurch, where the home we were given turned out to be a *barn*.

A stove and beds were brought in, but the building, located in the middle of a farm, was simply a barn with a high ceiling, and the walls inside were covered with tin sheets. Manure clinging on straw was stuck to those walls.

A bare light bulb hung from the high ceiling. I stood in the middle of this barn, which was to be home to our family of six, and couldn't hold back the tears. But remembering our current status, I knew there was no choice, that this was how it was, and would be, for some time yet. We regretted at that moment that we had not gone to Revelstoke, where a friend, Fukuyama Senkichi-san, had offered help, and there was even an occasion when my husband had gone to visit him for a week. But we had made this choice to come to Manitoba, and there was no way to change the decision. There is no remedy for a wrong decision once the decision is carried out.

My husband's oldest brother, Katsutaro-niisan, who had come earlier to Manitoba, soon dropped by and from that day began to work on the farm with us, weeding the onion patches and hoeing the tomato, lettuce and cauliflower fields, even though our luggage had not yet arrived.

The water that came out of the pump in Middlechurch was muddy and smelly. The children longed for the pure water of Minto and cried. [I was later told by a teacher in my Middlechurch school that even though the water smelled and was cloudy, it was not harmful and not to worry.] No amount of soap worked in laundering, so we learned to save rainwater or to haul water from the river nearby.

On the morning after our arrival, eleven-year-old Eiko and eight-year-old Toyoaki were assigned the job of looking after themselves and their little brother Kenji. Eiko was assigned to make sandwiches for lunch for all of us, and Toyoaki to haul water. My husband and I went to work on the farm, taking the youngest with us.

After we had worked six hours each day, Mr. Mancer would come around to hand out a bill from a roll of two-dollar bills. The truck was loaded with Ukrainian Canadian regular workers who were brought in each day from Winnipeg and returned. After working a whole day, to receive a daily wage of two dollars from Mr. Mancer—that is, to put my hand out servilely to receive it—was embarrassing for me, but with each day, I got used to the routine.

There was a German Mennonite family living on the same farm who left their single-unit house at the end of the summer, so we moved into this small two-storey house for the winter.

At this time, butter, sugar and rice were rationed. Since we had four small children, we had no shortage so we passed the rations on to those families working with us, all adults, who were lacking in rice rations.

Winter in Manitoba is severe, and to preserve the vegetables on this farm, Mr. Mancer had built a large underground storage space. Even in the wintertime, Ukrainian Canadian workers came to send products to market, but I remember one day there was no one working, so my husband told me to go into this storage area while he went to speak to Mr. Mancer to say we wished to buy some potatoes. I went with Eiko and we were packing the potatoes when Mr. Mancer appeared. He asked us if we always came here to take the potatoes, and I, instead of remaining silent, not understanding English and thinking he had asked if we wanted some potatoes, replied yes. For a moment, Mr. Mancer looked as though he might laugh. Eiko told him that Father had gone to Mr. Mancer's home to request permission and so we were waiting, and explained that her mother did not speak English.

This place, Middlechurch, was surrounded by large farms, and the school was located a distance away in town. Though our second son, who was now in grade one, walked along the highway to go to school with his older siblings, sometimes there was no class, so he returned home alone. On one such occasion, he said his ears were sore. I looked and found they were frozen. I had heard that the remedy was to rub the frozen parts with snow, so I rubbed his nose and ears with snow. The next day his ears were swollen. Because he did not pull his parka string tightly, likely the strong wind came through.

Every morning, the milkman delivered a huge bottle of milk, left by the telephone pole at the highway. Our older or our younger son, whoever awakened first, went to fetch the milk, which usually had an inch of frozen cream jutting out at the top. The first one to go to fetch the milk got to eat the frozen cream!

In those days, Japanese Canadians who had been farmers in British Columbia before the war were working at the Mancer farm in Middlechurch. They included the Yasumatsu couple, the Okano couple, the Ibukis, who were three with their son, and the Kitagawa couple, with a small child. Although they worked with us, I did not know whether they were living on Mancer's farm or commuting.

It is hard to imagine today that while Prime Minister Mackenzie King declared in the House of Commons that "it is a fact no person of Japanese race born in Canada has been charged with any act of sabotage or disloyalty during the years of war," another order was executed by him forcing Japanese Canadians either to repatriate to Japan (a country many had never known) or to disperse to points east of the Rockies, as the final solution. To justify this declaration of a "dispersal" policy, the prime minister said that "the sound policy and the best policy for the Japanese Canadians themselves is to distribute their numbers as widely as possible throughout the country where they will not create feelings of racial hostility."[4]

Japanese Canadians were blamed for causing racism. There was no need to question, for instance, why we had been living clustered, forming our own community, in downtown east-side Vancouver. Undoubtedly, this order was meant to ensure we did not return to resettle on the West Coast—what might be called ethnic cleansing, done to pacify or agree to the wishes and demands of the racists in the city of Vancouver and the province of British Columbia.

---

4   *House of Commons Debates*, August 4, 1944.

So it was illegal for Japanese Canadians to return to Vancouver or to the West Coast, despite the ending of the war.

Each time I read my mother's reaction to our new home, a *barn*, I get a lump in my throat and feel my eyes water. As a child turning twelve in the fall, I did not notice the reaction my mother had to this place, which perhaps is an indication that she kept any negative thoughts hidden from her children.

Perhaps, also, by this time I had little memory of what a "home" constituted, that is, the home we had left behind in Vancouver. Unlike the wealthy residents living in Minto, we had not brought sofas but sat on benches around the kitchen table, all built of raw wood. We had grown used to living with bare necessities and saw it as normal. Regardless of the fact that we lived in an old miner's house, one that had been dragged in from the outskirts for our use, it was our home. As a child, I had never thought about it as anything good or bad. I had never compared our home with those of my friends whose parents had brought furnishings and continued to live much as they had done in the past, even though I had visited them often, sitting on the sofa and singing songs with them while an older member of their family played the piano. I think that wherever children are, as long as they are supported by loving parents and siblings, that place is home.

In this, our new "home," the *barn*, we could hear the rustles of rats or mice among the straw in the attic. Since we had come directly to this place, and I don't remember being put up in a hotel, we must have begun living there even before it was properly cleaned out. Beds, a stove, tables and chairs (wooden benches), etc., had already been installed for our use, but I wonder now about bedding, since our baggage had not yet arrived. Likely we received help from Uncle Katsutaro, my father's oldest brother, who was living in Winnipeg at this time with his son, Yoshiyo, and his family, having moved to Manitoba earlier in 1942. As Mother writes, he soon moved in with us and worked with my parents.

My parents went to work on the farm almost immediately, Mother still wearing the beautiful dress that she had travelled in. I recall her saying she could always make another dress with the money she would be earning—hardly, when, with both parents working, they were each paid only two dollars a day!

We were resigned to living in the barn, having no choice in the matter, but at least we were told this was a temporary residence. Manitoba winters would not allow anyone to live in a building without proper insulation.

I often wonder now what people like Mr. Mancer, the farm owner, could have been thinking, or if they had any concern that we, a family of six with four young children, fellow human beings, Canadians (or did they not think of us as Canadians?), were treated in this way. The government called us "enemy aliens." And that is what we were, aliens, never having been offered the franchise (even as many families were already into their third generation, living in and contributing to Canada), not welcomed as citizens even as we were adding to the economy.

Of course, with the shortage of labour created by young men serving in the Canadian Forces, such farm owners were likely happy that the government was providing them with workers, with cheap labour. Probably they did not have much choice in the matter, but was this acceptable to Mr. Mancer? Did he and the other farmers (say, the owners of sugar beet farms where many Japanese Canadian families lived in even harsher conditions) have any conscience about this period?

⚬⚬

We had arrived in Middlechurch during summer. While my parents and my uncle Katsutaro worked in the vegetable fields, I, not yet twelve, was put in charge of my two brothers, just turned nine and six, and of preparing sandwiches for lunch for all of us. We were left on our own otherwise, my brothers chasing each other around the barn, isolated on this farm from any other children, though there might have been some in the neighbourhood. I recall making sandwiches with sliced Klik (canned meat, similar to Spam, which is still often spoken of by internees), eggs and fresh lettuce and tomatoes, served with some canned fruit.

My parents took my little sister, Keiko, now three, along to their work site. She stayed nearby while they hoed each row of the vegetable

garden. I remember Mother telling me that there were German prisoners of war working alongside them, each wearing a shirt with a large
red circle on the back, and that Father offered them cigarettes he had
rolled.

I learned years later, as I began to take interest in internment
history, that while 945 Japanese Canadian men were sent by the government to work on road construction at Blue River, Revelstoke, Hope,
Schreiber and Black Spur, those who complained about separation from
their families (notably the Nisei Mass Evacuation Group) were called
"dissidents" and approximately 699 men were sent to prisoner-of-war
camps at Angler and Petawawa in Ontario. They, too, were forced to
wear shirts with red circles on their backs.

When fall came, we moved into the house where the German
Mennonite family had previously lived. I don't know what happened
to them, but we heard that their son was in prison as a conscientious
objector, that is, a pacifist, refusing to take part in Canada's military
service.

In Middlechurch, my brothers and I had our first experience entering school in the larger society after having lived in the secluded internment site of Minto, where we all looked and acted as though we
were related.

From the first day of school, my brothers and I were treated as different, and we were made to feel inadequate in this new environment.
We were looked upon as objects of curiosity at best. Local students our
age were likely not aware of the reason why we were there, entering
their classrooms. And likely they had never, up to 1942, encountered
Asian faces. Little if any information about the internment, I'm sure,
was offered to schoolchildren (as is true in most schools even to this
day). All they knew about us was whatever their parents had shared
with them. And most parents, I assume, received their information
through the media—radio and newspapers that never reported about
us kindly in those days.

My class consisted of several grades, with one teacher teaching all
subjects. When I arrived, the classroom already had two Nisei students,
Kay Yasumatsu and Norman Ibuki. They were older, I believe in grade

eight or nine, while I was entering grade six, and they looked and acted settled, quite confident. Likely their parents had opted to move to this area in 1942, perhaps to work on sugar beet farms, while we had moved to Minto. And so they were already adapted to the situation.

My teacher, Mr. B, had difficulty pronouncing my name, Eiko. He did not try, and he stumbled over it whenever he spoke to me in class. I could, today, be more charitable and say that words beginning with *ei* could be pronounced as *ai*, and that was why he often called me Ayoka, or some such pronunciation. But I believe it was incumbent on him, as a teacher, to treat his students with respect, at least to learn how to pronounce their names correctly, and not treat them as strange beings. I have since learned that in many schools during the dispersal period, students moving into Canada's public school system were told to give themselves English names.

Returning home after each such incident, mortified, often crying that it was bad enough that I looked different but having the teacher stumble over the pronunciation of my name added further attention and embarrassment, I told Mother it was just too much to bear. Mother finally said, "Let's give you an English name for the new term." Mother, who did not speak English, remembered two people from her past life in Vancouver, women she respected as accomplished. Their names were Lily and Grace. She said, and I agreed, that I was no lily, so for the next school term, I was registered as Grace.

I have since often wondered with regret about my self-centredness, my ignorance in not thinking about how my younger brothers were faring in those days. I thought only of my own discomfort and receiving Mother's attention and sympathies. Mother had no brothers, and I realize now that she had little experience or knowledge about boys, let alone raising sons. She had married at the young age of eighteen and had become a mother soon after. Father was more often than not working away from home, wherever a job was available. This was especially true while we lived in Middlechurch, since there was no farm work during the winter months.

The younger of my two brothers, Kenji, started school without having the benefit of a kindergarten experience. Toyoaki, the older, was nine. His name changed to Tom in time, but I recall seeing him in schoolyard fights, with classmates calling him "Tayo Wacky." I don't remember him complaining at home, as I did. Undoubtedly, he was experiencing some difficult times, but he was not able to share this with Mother (or with our always absent Father) as I, his older sister, a girl, was doing, and receiving sympathy.

We lived a quarter of a mile away from the school and walked there and back, whether in good weather or in bad winter conditions. On many such days, upon returning home, we would say to Mother, "We were so lucky. On the way home we were picked up by a car." And Mother would respond, "I'm so happy. There are always some good people."

In those days, whenever a car stopped to offer us a ride, we jumped in. Obviously, there were many good people around who treated us not as "Japs" but only as children, as we reached our destination safely.

Most parents today don't allow their children to walk even a few blocks to school on their own, never mind a quarter of a mile on the highway, and not to mention happily jumping into a stranger's car. For Mother, it was not just about being naive; with Father working away from Middlechurch during the winter months, she had no choice but to put her trust in her oldest child to keep the younger ones safe, and to trust humankind there in rural Manitoba.

My sensitivity around the issue of difference was likely exacerbated by an incident that happened just before I started school. When my parents were unable to work on the farm because of rain, Mother and I sometimes took the highway bus into the city of Winnipeg—it was not far—to do some shopping at Eaton's. (Those of us who had been dispersed to the east of the Rockies were not yet allowed to live in the city.) I always looked forward to this trip with Mother. An excellent seamstress, she would spend time in the pattern book section of Eaton's and then go to the fabric department to look for sales for her next sewing project. Or we would go to the basement, where fresh fish could be purchased. We likely bought mackerel, which was not too expensive. In those days, we had no fridge to preserve raw fish, so the mackerel, marinated, would be turned into sushi for dinner, made special by our favourite uncle's presence.

On one occasion, as we boarded the bus, we encountered a young boy, not much older than I, yelling loudly to his mother, "Look, Mom, there's a Jap!" This was my first experience of publicly being brought to attention for the way we looked.

I did not fully comprehend the ramifications at the time. However, the humiliation I felt that day would live with me for many years to come. I was not yet aware of the word *racism*. Inadequacy was what I felt in my interactions with students and teachers. I was not good enough, not one of *them*, which had already been confirmed outside of the classroom. Years later, I would read a more eloquent telling of such an incident by Frantz Fanon in his book *Black Skins, White Masks*.

Once, Father made the effort to take our family to the Starland Theatre in Winnipeg to see a movie titled *The Sullivans* about five brothers who fought and lost their lives in the Pacific War. It was a sad story, and I find it surprising, thinking back to that day, that we bused into Winnipeg to see the film. Why had Father chosen this movie for us to see? Was it about the futility of war?

While undoubtedly some Issei believed Japan could not lose the war (looking back perhaps to the Russo-Japanese War of 1904 or perhaps to their warrior/samurai tradition), most, believing themselves to be Canadians (even without the franchise), worried about what would happen to us when the war was over. Second-generation or Nisei men had tried to enlist to fight on behalf of Canada, to show loyalty, but they had not been allowed. It was not until the war was coming to an end, when the British military under Admiral Mountbatten, first Earl Mountbatten of Burma, requested that Japanese Canadians enlist as corporals to offer interpreting and translation services in Burma, that the Canadian government finally assented under pressure. About a hundred young Nisei men enlisted in the Canadian military, their ranks reduced from corporals to privates.

Mother, while especially fearful about what might happen to us next since our grandmother and her first daughter were living in Japan and we had little knowledge about them as all mail was censored at this time, never believed Japan could win the war. As she suggested quietly at home, how could a country that had, until recently, been fighting with bamboo sticks and swords expect to win against Western military powers that had long been engaged in building huge arsenals and for centuries had been colonizing throughout the world?

Our life in Middlechurch was acknowledged from the beginning as temporary. It was a given that my parents had to find another location where Father could access a job that paid enough to properly support and care for us into the future. A total of four dollars a day, with both of them working on the farm, was not enough for us even to subsist as a family of six. To boot, there was no work and therefore no pay on rainy days or during the winter months. So when Father was informed by friends that work was available at a company called Moss Spur, we moved to the neighbouring town of Whitemouth, east along the highway.

WAR ENDS BUT RESTRICTIONS CONTINUE

Mother:

On August 15, 1945, the war ended. We were picking rasp-
berries in the field when Mr. Mancer came to inform us that
Japan had surrendered and there were great celebrations
taking place in the city of Winnipeg. When we were living
in Minto, we had listened to the radio so we kept up somewhat with the war situation. But here, on this farm, hearing
about an unconditional surrender, and thinking about the
Japanese people, including mother, daughter and relatives,
we were for a time speechless.

Even in quarrels, never mind wars, one side has to win
before the quarrel ends. For those of us who lived in a country that labelled us "enemy aliens" even though we were
naturalized Canadians, we had to endure the hardship. We
worked with our hands in the vegetable garden, with German war prisoners wearing uniforms with a red circle on
their backs.

That year, winter passed and even though the war had
ended, we were not yet allowed to move into the city.

We found a rental in a place called Whitemouth, and
we waited until spring 1946 to leave Mancer's farm. It was
a small town, located about the same distance east as Winnipeg was to the west from Middlechurch. There was a
school and a hotel, and we rented the back half of Mr. Ernie
Webb's garage. My husband got a job at a moss-gathering
company (Moss Spur) and later at a lumber mill in Dryden,
Ontario. I looked after the children and made use of the

seamstress instructions I had received in Vancouver, taking dressmaking and alteration jobs from the townspeople. While in Minto, I had also taken design classes once a week from Mrs. Watada, who had been taught in Vancouver at the Kawano dressmaking school.

People in the neighbourhood were very kind to us here in Whitemouth, and one of them lent us a washing machine. The children went to school and on Sundays went to the United Church. In those days, Miss Lois Freeman, a young student minister, commuted from Winnipeg and gave guidance to Eiko and to others her age in town.

In this town there was Oye Asako-san and her four sons, and a daughter married to Sakai Kiyoshi-san, with their three children. They lived together in a large house not too far from us. And there was Hayakawa-san, with a family of five or six. Although the town was small, there were shops on the main street and a school nearby with several classrooms.

There was a railway station where farmers took their products to send to markets. The trains had large numbers of freight cars attached to them. Living on the prairies, we were able to enjoy the spectacle of a train moving along the wide horizon, and I more than once found myself counting the cars: *ichi, ni, san, shi, go* [one, two, three, four, five] ...

One day in Whitemouth, we received a rare visit. Hamade Itsuji-san, Doi Mataichiro-san and Nishimura Hideo-san were on a mission to open a Buddhist temple in Winnipeg. Nishimura Hideo-san, who knew the Buddhist sutra well, decided that a temple should be built there. I quickly informed Oye-san, Sakai-san and Hayakawa-san, and we all gathered at our home, using apple boxes as extra chairs.

When Nishimura Hideo-san began reciting a sutra, at each interval he would hit the bell, and there was a gale of laughter from the children, who had never experienced such a service. I believe this was the first introduction to Buddhism in Manitoba.

Hamade-san eventually moved back to British Columbia.

For me, who had lost my mother when I was only seventeen, for the first time since coming to Canada I remembered the past with nostalgic longing, and I found myself sitting before the *butsudan* [portable shrine] every night, remembering my father, Yamamoto Fukumatsu, and my two living sisters, while reciting the "Shoshin Nembutsu Ge," a sutra I had memorized.

Yes, the war had ended in 1945. Yet we were not allowed freedom, still not allowed to return to the West Coast, where in any case there was no home to return to. All personal property, everything left behind, had been confiscated by the government as early as the first year of internment and sold without the owners' consent.

Japanese Americans, in accordance with the Constitution of the United States (anyone born in the United States was a full citizen), had been sent to concentration camps, incarcerated behind barbed wire fences and guarded by the military. Yet, as the war was ending, they were freed and allowed to return to the West Coast beginning in early 1945. Japanese Canadians were forced to continue their journey as outcasts, as aliens, not Canadians. We had no homes to return to.

When we moved to Whitemouth in 1946, Father was able to rent the second floor of a house owned by a kind Ukrainian immigrant couple, Mr. and Mrs. Chleborob. But soon, not finding the rental space adequate, we moved into a large three-room space behind a service station owned by Mr. Ernie Webb, at the edge of town, leading onto the main highway. The space was not the best but at least it was on the main floor with private back-door access. The Webb family, who lived next door, were very kind to us, offering Mother an old wringer-type washing machine they had replaced with a newer model. Mother was very grateful, as at this time she was still using the scrub board in an aluminum tub with Sunlight soap.

As Mother writes, at least four other Japanese Canadian families had already moved to Whitemouth as a result of the government's new order. One family she refers to lived just a short walk from our home. The grandmother, Mrs. Asako Oye, was the wife of the fisherman who had been found with his tongue slit after a major search along the West Coast when he and his boat went missing in 1942.

Mrs. Oye visited Mother weekly, still grieving over this unresolved loss. I had often wondered if the family members made any attempt to see if the government had investigated his death, so I recently contacted a granddaughter living in Winnipeg to inquire. She kindly sent me a copy of the coroner's report, a sparse document that records only that he committed suicide through asphyxiation at the hospital. Apparently, he had removed the life support himself. There is no explanation in this report regarding his condition when he was brought to the hospital after his boat was found. Such a heartbreaking event obviously did not concern the government of that time, or any later one. It appears that no investigation was done.

I remember the more than three years we spent in the community of Whitemouth largely as positive. This is where I turned into a teenager. This is where, for the first time, I more naturally interacted with community residents and made school friends.

I have memories of kind and generous people in Whitemouth, not the stares I had received in Middlechurch, where only Mary Sarna, a classmate, had made an attempt to be a friend, even visiting me at my home. She had no fear of crossing the highway to visit with us. I did not at that time have the courage to make friends, however, always feeling like an outsider. I remember that on one of Mary's visits, we sat and ate the delicious apples my uncle Konosuke, living in Vernon at that time, had sent us from the Chiba farm where he was working. While we were moving east of the Rockies, to Manitoba, Uncle Konosuke was preparing to return to his wife and family, that is, to be repatriated to Japan, under the government's new dispersal/repatriation order.

One of the many happy events I experienced upon moving to Whitemouth was meeting the young and attractive daughter of the rail station master, who had been working and living away but had just returned to her family home. Besides being the first young white woman that I could comfortably face and speak to directly, she took an interest in me. She likely recognized in me someone without self-confidence, wishing to belong, and offered me clothes from her not-too-distant past. There were two stylish, hardly worn suits, one blue and the other gold in colour, made of soft wool fabric, which I proudly and happily wore to church and to special events, and a white zippered jacket that I wore with pride and that offered me confidence as I skated at the outdoor community rink. As a teenager with little help from immigrant parents to participate in current trends, I was thrilled beyond words.

Mother's design sense was nothing short of excellent, as she was always looking through the magazines she found and doing her best to make sure I was dressed properly, sometimes too much so. But I felt ecstatic to wear *store-bought* clothes that a young, stylish woman had originally chosen for herself.

The town itself had all the amenities, such as a large grocery store that sold some clothing, a hardware store (the owner's daughter Anita, a classmate, became my best friend) and a café run by a local attorney's wife, Mrs. Peterson, where I would later get a job serving. And, of course, there was a bank and a hotel.

I participated in various activities, joining the United Church choir and the CGIT, Canadian Girls in Training, formed by a student minister, Lois Freeman, who some years later became moderator of the United Church of Canada. She travelled to Whitemouth from Winnipeg by motorbike to hold the weekly Sunday service.

Ms. Freeman introduced me to the board chair of the United Church in Whitemouth, Mrs. Wardrop, who appointed me to attend the United Church conference, held in Winnipeg, as the local representative. I believe this was at Ms. Freeman's behest. I was invited to stay for the weekend at her parents' home, the Manse; her father was the minister of Crescent Fort Rouge United Church and also dean of theology at United College (later the University of Winnipeg). It was the first time I had visited the city of Winnipeg other than my brief shopping excursions to Eaton's with Mother from Middlechurch. While I was careful to attend the conference meetings so that I might offer a proper report upon my return to Whitemouth, Ms. Freeman kindly took time to ensure my visit included some enjoyment of the city—at that time, for me, a totally foreign world.

I remember Rev. Lois Freeman as one of the first people to help me in overcoming the unease and timidity of an outsider in social contact with an unfamiliar culture. I was to meet her again many years later at a peace conference in Vancouver.

Socially, for the first time since leaving Minto, my brothers and I began spending time with new friends, watching hockey games at the local rink and, in my case, visiting neighbouring towns like Lac du Bonnet. I learned to skate, spending many evenings at the community skating rink, and even to square dance at town hall events. A couple of years later, I joined the town curling club and our team placed third in a competition, winning each player the prize of a fancy bedroom lamp. This was a memorable experience for me. Not only had I been invited to curl with town folks and been on one of the winning teams, but, with no frills in our home, just bare necessities, we now had a beautiful lamp in our bedroom.

Still restricted in his movement, not yet having the freedom or economic stability to select a permanent residence, Father moved from job to job, wherever one was available. He was soon working at the Dryden Paper Mill in Ontario, where many Japanese Canadian men had already been hired. Mother was focused on saving as much as possible while we awaited the next order from the government and whatever new restrictions it might constitute.

Again, I have little memory of what my two brothers were doing, how they were adjusting; I was given the task only of ensuring they returned home on time for dinner each day. I was focused on overcoming my own insecurities. I turned thirteen in the fall of the year we moved to Whitemouth, and I should have been more aware. In later years, when I had gained the confidence to think back to that time, I wondered what my siblings must have been dealing with. There is no doubt in my mind that things could not have been easy for Toyoaki (now Tom). He was ten when we moved to Whitemouth and Kenji was only seven.

While I shared with Mother the problems I was enduring, especially since I was helping her in the kitchen daily, tidying after each meal and babysitting my little sister, Tom seldom if ever looked to her for help. Father was not available to offer guidance. During those years, we children had little connection to our father; he came and went, spending every other weekend with us, always smiling and happy to see us. Mother cooked special meals on those very special weekends, usually freshly killed chicken bought at a nearby farm, cooked in sukiyaki sauce, since beef was not accessible to us in those days.

Tom, like me, found this new environment of Whitemouth friendly. A classmate who lived on a nearby farm invited him to help with farm chores. Of course, to be fair, while in Middlechurch, we had not had the opportunity to interact much with classmates, as we lived a distance away from the townsite and were there for only a year or so. Our only experience of interaction with classmates was in the classroom or the schoolyard.

However, there were indications of Tom's struggles as we began our lives in Whitemouth. One incident shortly after we moved there sticks in my memory. As we lined up one morning after the bell rang to be marched into the school, Tom was being disciplined by a teacher. He must have done something to arouse the ire of Mr. W, who was supervising us. From the line I was standing in, I could see the elderly teacher scolding him. Without hesitation, I rushed over to Mr. W in defence of my brother. I don't remember what exactly I said to him, but he looked at me sternly and told me to return to my line. He did not further discipline my brother. But I came to respect Mr. W as my homeroom teacher. He daily urged me to work hard and to move forward. I felt that as a German Canadian teacher, he understood the circumstances of history that had led us to this town.

Whitemouth was where I slowly but surely began to feel like part of a community and a culture different from that experienced in our home. The town's residents were Canadians of various backgrounds: some British living in town and running businesses and also people largely of German, Mennonite and eastern European backgrounds, some owning businesses but mostly farm families. Through them, I was able to expand my own interests and possibilities as a Canadian, something they, without losing their ethnicities, took for granted.

It was there in Whitemouth that one day I asked my mother if I could take piano lessons. I was already taking part in the local United Church choir. Singing was something Mother and I did daily, mainly Japanese songs she had taught me, particularly as we washed and dried the dinner dishes together.

While in Minto, I had felt like a misfit as my classmates, mostly children from pre-war established middle-class families, sang songs from the *Hit Parade*, which they had access to through the radios and phonographs they had brought with them. Not having older siblings to learn from, I was not aware of the currently popular songs. And of course Mother, who had come to Canada only a dozen years or so before internment, was raising her children as a Japanese mother, with little knowledge of Canadian culture or customs, including the language, let alone popular songs in English. The only English-language songs I knew were those I learned in the classroom.

I had never studied music, and none of my friends in Whitemouth seemed particularly interested in it. But I remember pleading

When the family moved to Whitemouth from Middlechurch, Grace and her siblings began to socialize with others their age, also from diverse backgrounds. Posed on the Whitemouth High School steps are Shirley Carlson, Shirley Jorgenson, Lleana Giesbrecht, Connie Aitkenhead, and Claire Sinclair, close friends of Grace's, in 1948-49.

with Mother once I learned that the piano installed at Whitemouth's town hall, where lessons were offered weekly by a visiting piano teacher, could also be used by students for their daily practice.

Piano lessons were probably the last thing my parents would have thought to offer us children. After all, we were living in a time when we were still worried about our daily survival and about what the next order from the government might be. Close to three years after the end of the war, we were still living as "aliens" without civil liberties.

However, Mother was very aware of what her children were missing in life. I'm sure this was related to her upbringing in Japan, which she had not forgotten, and I believe she wanted us to experience some dignity. After much consideration, she decided that she could afford the lessons for me. Father had his job in Dryden, so there was regular income. Also, Mother was herself earning money, as word went out into the community that she was a seamstress.

I was in seventh heaven as I began attending classes under Mrs. Jorgenson, the local music teacher. On weekdays, I happily went and practised after school.

However, my joy was not to last. One day, after only a couple of months of daily practice, as I was leaving the hall, the town clerk, a man who looked to be over sixty years of age, much older than my parents, grabbed me and forced himself on me, kissing me. I extricated myself and ran out of the building—and, of course, immediately quit the lessons.

At fourteen, living in a cultural environment I was not yet sure of, I didn't know how to handle this. I did not tell anyone about the experience or make any attempt to pursue other avenues for continuing the lessons.

Mother, understandably, expressed both anger and disappointment. She had expected much more effort on my part. She never forgave me for quitting so soon after I had begun, especially after I had made such an issue of wanting to take the lessons. From that day forward, piano lessons were never mentioned, and that was the end of any musical ambitions I might have had.

But what could I have done? It was a repeat of what had happened to me in Minto, except that in Whitemouth Mother had no power of language or position, while in Minto exposing the incident would have been more a matter of cultural shame.

Though generously accepted by its residents, we were in fact un-invited guests in Whitemouth, not to mention that we were still un-der government restrictions, watched over by the RCMP. How could we speak against the community's possibly well-respected town clerk? And what would have happened had I told my new friends and their parents? When I look back, I think that I should have at least told my music teacher or consulted with my church friends. But instead, I hid the whole incident and buried it within a past I hoped I would forget but never did.

Our years in Whitemouth ended with our move to Winnipeg in 1950. My classmates held a special farewell event for me at Whitemouth High School, where I had just begun my first year. I remember with nostalgia their gift of a small suitcase, along with a speech offered by my classmate Billy Aitkenhead, whose sister, Connie, was also a classmate and a good friend. The other classmates I remember best are Clara Sin-clair, John Paulson and of course my best friend, Anita Hill.

I remember these years in Whitemouth, from 1946 to 1950, as happy ones. However, as was the case when I left Minto, after leaving I did not look back, did not keep contact with my new friends, faced with the reality of once again dealing with a new environment, this time a city and a large city school.

PART TWO

To Winnipeg

Race as a ground for exclusion from the federal vote was, at long last, repealed from the Dominion Elections Act in 1948, and the right to vote was extended to all Canadians of Asian origin. Japanese Canadians were able to vote in the provincial elections of 1949.

After much political infighting, the order-in-council that had prohibited our return to the West Coast was repealed by the government, and on April 1, 1949, Japanese Canadians were finally given civil liberties, that is, full freedom of movement as Canadian citizens.

That meant we were finally allowed to return. But after having been forced under the dispersal order to relocate to the east of the Rockies even after the war had ended in 1945, my parents, now living in rural Manitoba, made the decision not to return but to resettle in the city of Winnipeg.

Their move was not a matter of choice. The decision reflected their depleted financial condition. There could be no consideration of moving back to Vancouver, where they had begun their lives in Canada with great hope. In any event, there was no home to return to. No job for my father to return to. Everything they had owned prior to 1942 was gone, confiscated by the government or stolen and sold at auctions. The only choice they had was to remain in Manitoba, where they would hopefully find work to begin a new life raising their four school-aged children and also making arrangements to bring home their first child, my older sister, Kikuko, who had been living in Japan with our grandmother for more than a decade by then.

At least Winnipeg was familiar to Father. He had lived there as a young man and had enjoyed working at the railway hotel, the Royal Alexandra, before his marriage. My parents' only worry was whether discrimination would continue in Winnipeg and whether that would be a factor in looking for home and work opportunities.

When we moved into the city, we were advised by our own community leaders to remember the prime minister's urgings that Japanese Canadians should disperse throughout the country so as not to "create feelings of racial hostility."

We were warned not to form ethnic neighbourhoods with total disregard for the fact that this had happened in Vancouver because we were a discriminated-against community of immigrants, though my parents were naturalized Canadians with Canadian-born children. Even with some families already moving into the third generation, we had still been treated as foreigners or, worse, "aliens," and were refused Canadian citizenship even as we were contributing to the economy.

In Winnipeg, we were advised to "distribute" ourselves among already existing neighbourhoods, often clusters of specific European ethnic communities that, we quickly learned, carried their own memories of discrimination. About three hundred Japanese Canadian families moved into Winnipeg at this time, all focused on looking for work and homes in a new environment that was not altogether welcoming at first.

Mother remembers:

Hirayama "Happy"-san, already living in Winnipeg, helped us to lease a large house in which the rooms we did not need for our own family use could be rented out for income. Our youngest daughter, Keiko, with support from the older ones, began attending school, and my husband, again with Happy-san's assistance, was hired by a tannery where several other Japanese Canadians had already found work. As for me, I began working in a garment factory.

On the first morning of commuting, I was struck by the large number of people going to work, which gave me courage. I was amazed at the number of people working in the factory, making parkas. Pattern marks were drawn with chalk on the top layer of cloth, piled ten to twelve deep on a table and then cut out. Some seamstresses sewed the hoods, and only the hoods. Some sewed the jacket, some did the finishing and some put in the buttonholes. Until we got used to the work, we were put on timework pay, and as soon as speed was achieved, we went to piecework. I sewed parkas, blue jeans, jackets and even men's shirts.

Every morning I left for work with a kerchief on my head. It was the coldest when the weather dropped below zero. In those days, buses burned coal as fuel. Someone like me, wearing glasses, had to deal with glasses fogging up on entering the bus after standing in the cold waiting. For a moment, I would be blinded. I wonder now when the buses changed to other fuel.

Once, after working overtime until seven, I was taking the bus to go to Daniel McIntyre High School, where I was taking English-language lessons. I was holding the bus fare change in my wool glove, but when the bus came and I boarded, I found I was short twenty cents, which must have dropped from my glove while I was waiting. The bus driver very kindly said it was okay, told me to hurry in and sit down and allowed me to ride. I have never forgotten this kind incident.

In this way, I spent two years studying beginner's English. I learned to pronounce words but had difficulty with meaning. Once I returned home, we would be speaking in Japanese, and so I continued to depend on my children's support. I think this was my biggest mistake in life, that I did not take myself more seriously.

I remember Mother beginning her new life in this city with great expectations. Her first thought was to learn to speak English to catch up to her children, even though she was spending long hours doing piecework in the garment factory. After all, everyone around her spoke English, and although she could by this time understand some parts of the conversation, I'm sure she wanted to gain more independence through language.

I don't believe she was "too old to learn," as she told us when she quit taking classes, or that she did not take herself seriously, as she cites with regret in her memoir. She was likely just too tired by the end of each day, even though she was, at the beginning, committed to this effort.

For the first time in years, my parents appeared to be happy as they settled in to the city of Winnipeg and began working not only to survive but, I believe, to fulfill their long-postponed dreams.

⁓

In 1950, Winnipeg experienced a devastating flood, which Mother describes in her memoir:

> The basement of our home was filled with water from the sewer pipes. In the middle of the basement was a large furnace, and even though we shovelled coal in to keep the fire burning to heat the house, the furnace had become waterlogged. It looked as though we would have to wait until the water receded.
>
> However, one day when I returned home from work, the company that employed my husband, Sterling, had sent some men over, and a machine was pumping out the water. I realized then that no matter where we went, there were always people who rescued us with kindness.
>
> Two families who lived in the house as our tenants had to experience the cold in the house for a while, but the basement was soon returned to normal, with the furnace functioning properly again.

Mother had become actively engaged with committee members of the Manitoba Buddhist Temple, which was already established and had various ongoing activities. She learned from her new friends that young Japanese Canadians were volunteering to help at the flood sites with sandbagging, and she encouraged me to join them. Up until then, I had met only a couple of young people through family friends, so this was my first opportunity to connect with the community.

Although I did take part in sandbagging and made some new friends, at that time, I gave little thought to any social life. I did not feel comfortable among young people, especially when most were a little older and seemingly already assimilated into the developing Japanese Canadian community, through social activity groups, and into the larger society as well. I was still focused on resettling with my siblings, each of us dealing for the first time with having to register in large city schools.

Upon arriving in Winnipeg, I had been introduced to a high school in the north end, St. John's Technical High School, by Ai Otsu, whose family was already settled in the city. (She, being older than me, was soon to move to a teaching job in Norway House, in northern Manitoba, after attending normal school.) Ai was the daughter of Mr. Genji Otsu, Uncle Konosuke's fisher friend from pre-war Steveston.

The students at St. John's were largely Jewish, but I also met students of Scandinavian, Ukrainian and Polish ancestries. Interestingly, when I come to think of it, we were very much aware of one another's ethnicity in those days.

Though I was fortunate in being introduced to this high school by Ai, it was a traumatic experience to attend a large city school when I had until then been taught mainly in classrooms containing several grades, often with one instructor teaching all subjects. My new school was filled with students who confidently debated subjects with the teachers. It is not far-fetched to say I felt like someone arriving from a foreign country having to learn the English alphabet for the first time. Even taking part in physical education class was a new experience, as I knew nothing about basketball, volleyball or ballroom dancing.

St. John's Tech was located some distance away over the Salter Bridge from our rental home at 287 Isabel Street. To avoid the daily cost of taking a bus, my parents bought me my first bicycle.

My siblings were registered in schools nearby, with the youngest, Keiko, now in grade two. I was charged once again with ensuring they returned home safely each day and also with beginning dinner preparation before Mother and Father got home from their respective workplaces.

As Mother indicates in her memoir, fortunately, help with settling was available from members of our community. Several families who likely spent the internment years working on Manitoba's sugar beet farms had arrived first and were already established in the city of Win-

nipeg, and among them community leaders had emerged.
They were mostly older Nisei,
versed in both English and Japanese, who offered support to
newcomers. The names Mother recalls in her memoir were
Harold Hirose, Shinji Sato and
Happy Hirayama, among others. Mr. Hirayama assisted my
parents in getting us the home
we were able to rent.

Harold Hirose was well
respected in the national community. When the federal government on July 13, 1947, established a Royal Commission, led
by Justice Henry Bird, to hold
hearings on property losses
and to recommend compen-
sation for qualified claimants,

A newspaper clipping depicting one of
the multicultural events Grace took part in
during her teens; despite the message of
acceptance demonstrated by these events,
Grace was very aware of the prejudice her
family, along with other cultural groups and
ethnicities, continued to face. Author's personal collection

the Manitoba Japanese Canadian Citizens' Association, formed in 1946,
created a Property Loss Committee. Mr. Hirose chaired this committee, with Saul Cherniack as legal counsel. (A member of the Legisla-
tive Assembly of Manitoba from 1962 to 1981, Mr. Cherniack served as
a cabinet minister in the NDP government of Ed Schreyer, who later
was appointed Governor General.) Hearings were held in April 1948 in
Manitoba, but not surprisingly, they ended with little being offered by
the government.

There are many stories of Japanese Canadians who had moved to
Winnipeg being refused the rental of advertised spaces and also jobs
because of continuing discriminatory practices. However, there were
also many kind and generous offers, in particular from the Jewish community in Winnipeg, of homes and jobs during this period. My parents
rented their large house from a Jewish landlord, Father was hired by

a Jewish-owned company, Sterling Fur, and Mother worked in a Jewish-owned garment factory.

I didn't realize it as a teenager, but Jews faced serious discrimination themselves at the time. In the early 1960s, while I was employed by a major law firm in Winnipeg as a legal secretary, I would find out something that shocked me.

One day when the law firm partners were holding a farewell party at a private club for a member of their firm, I was surprised to notice one lawyer still in his office. I asked why he was not at the party, and I will never forget his answer: "Why would I go to a party being held at a place where normally we are not allowed?" Jews were excluded from membership at such professional clubs, I discovered, and that was not all. I soon learned that Jews were also excluded from purchasing homes in certain areas of Winnipeg.

Harold Hirose also was a veteran of the Second World War, one of the Nisei men who responded to the British Army's request for Japanese Canadians to enlist and serve as interpreters in Southeast Asia toward the end of the war.

Among others who enlisted was Aki, the young son of Shinji Sato. Undoubtedly, enlistment was not an easily made decision. These young men, born in Canada but not offered citizenship, wishing to show loyalty to Canada and hoping in time to be accepted as full-fledged Canadian citizens, joined the war forces to fight against fascism while leaving behind their naturalized Canadian parents and their siblings, who were held in various internment sites as "enemy aliens."

I am still moved and filled with admiration when I read Shinji Sato's address to his community regarding his son's decision to enlist:

> I am in full accord with my son's decision because I realize that it is best for his future. ... His future means your future, our future, the future of all Canadians of Japanese ancestry. There are some Issei who think that such an act is treachery on our part. I do not think so. At odd moments when I have dwelled on the fact that we are taking arms against the land of our origin, I have uneasy moments. This is because

I know Japan more intimately than you Nisei do. There are many good things about Japan and there are many great people in Japan who have contributed to world knowledge of which I will always be proud. Yet, we must fight against them. In my opinion our war against Japan is not a war to abolish the Japanese civilization, but to protect it from Fascist doctrine and to establish a democratic government for the coming generation in Japan.[5]

Other Nisei veterans identified are George Higa, Tom Hoshizaki, Klark Ito, Jim Matsuo, Elmer Oike, Bill Sasaki and Goro Suzuki.

In my later teen years, when I began doing volunteer work with the Manitoba Japanese Canadian Citizens' Association, I would meet and be educated by the same Shinji Sato, who kindly introduced me to cross-cultural aspects of Winnipeg, teaching me about cultural and political groupings and their histories, particularly those of eastern European immigrants.

This new way (for me) of viewing society as consisting of human beings, rather than just whites and Asians living in opposition, would become my focus in understanding my own position as I began working in the larger world alongside various others.

---

5   Manitoba Japanese Canadian Citizens' Association, *The History of Japanese Canadians in Manitoba* (Winnipeg: Manitoba Japanese Canadian Citizens' Association, 1996), 65.

KIKUKO RETURNS

Mother:

My oldest daughter, who had been with my mother-in-law in Japan, had daily, together with classmates, been walking a distance of two *ri* [eight kilometres] to attend high school. Just like in Canada, since the end of the war the school had changed to a three-three system, and it was announced that those who continued for an extra year would be awarded a graduation certificate. Some students quit and went to work. Others continued, but those who returned were few. My mother-in-law wrote to inform us of the costs of going to school and asked that a bicycle be sent to our daughter.

At that time, as luck would have it, there was a family in Whitemouth who in 1946, in response to the government's new decree, decided to go to Japan. We asked them to take the bicycle for us. The bicycle arrived safely and my daughter was able to ride the two *ri* to and from school.

We learned at this time that during the war, American planes had flown over my mother-in-law's village in Japan and machine guns had been fired so that there were many times when the countryside was turned upside down.

On February 11, 1951, our daughter Kikuko, now nineteen years and three months old, together with our nephews Nishikihama Teruo, twenty-three, and Nishikihama Yoshiharu, twenty-four, departed from Yokohama to return to Canada. My mother-in-law and my sister, Hideyo, saw them off.

At long last our daughter was returning home to Canada. In those days, airplanes were not accessible, so my second

Kikuko remained in Japan for the duration of the war. In 1946, Sawae arranged to send a bicycle to her eldest daughter, so she could continue her education by travelling more easily to a distant school. Author's personal collection

daughter, Eiko, went to Vancouver by train to meet her. We went to Winnipeg's train station to greet them.

Since this child left, I had wondered why I had allowed this to happen, why I had let her go, and regretted this and cried every night. In my dreams of her, she was as at the time of her departure, only eight years of age. Although I had thought I would hold her tightly when she returned, of course the person who came off the train in Winnipeg was a young woman. She came to me to be embraced, but I hesitated for a moment. I have come to realize that the coldness she showed toward me throughout the rest of her life was a result of this moment of hesitation on my part. I forever regretted that I could not turn the clock back to replay this moment.

Raised as an only child by my mother-in-law, Kikuko found in Canada four siblings who spoke English, and I was totally involved in raising the youngest child. She took to going into her own room and writing *tanka* or haiku [Japanese poetry]. Indeed, she was feeling lonely and I felt sorry for her but didn't know what to do.

While studying English, she took up hairdressing, and with perseverance she began speaking more fluently with her siblings. She worked during the day and taught Japanese at the Buddhist church Japanese-language school in the evenings.

Eventually, we moved out of the rental house to buy a home of our own in 1953.

I seem to have blanked from my memory the pre-war years I spent in Vancouver with my sister. I have little recollection of being in kindergarten, which was the time my sister left us. I do remember walking with her. As the older sister by two years, she always put one arm protectively around my shoulders. But beyond that, I don't remember much about our relationship. It must have been traumatic for me, at about five or six years of age, not only to find her gone all of a sudden but also to have to replace her to become the big sister myself soon after.

Mother told me that Grandmother had asked for the opportunity to meet her grandchildren. Since we had relatives going to Japan at the time, my parents had initially decided to send my sister and me for a visit under their care. However, apparently I cried and said I didn't want to go. I'm told I was a bit of a *nakimiso* (crybaby) in those days. In a family portrait taken just before Nēchan (older sister) left, she and I are wearing the matching clothes Mother had made for our departure. Mother had also purchased a coat and hat for each of us.

I learned years later that it was not a strange thing in those days to send a child not only to visit but also to live with relatives in Japan. In fact, many children were sent to Japan to be educated, considering the situation in Canada, where there was no hope without franchise of a professional job, even with higher education. The parents remained in Canada, focused on making money and expecting to return home one day.

Nēchan, also called Kiku-chan, had been sent with our relatives for a short visit, but she was not to return to us until 1951, when the government granted permission after investigation into our family's financial situation.

I was sent to meet my sister in Vancouver, since both my parents were working and could not afford to take time off. Thinking back, I'm amazed at how trusting my parents were, sending an unworldly seventeen-year-old on a train from Winnipeg to Vancouver, a two-night journey by coach. Treated as the oldest of four children, I was perhaps looked upon as more responsible than my age would indicate. And, of course, there was no choice in the matter. The train was full of Canadian soldiers not much older than me. Fortunately, they were considerate and friendly, and I recall chatting with a couple of them.

A Japanese travel agency, Iwata Travel in East Vancouver, looked after the details of her return passage, and my sister and I spent her first night in Canada in a hotel arranged by the agency. Though my memories are vague, I know I was very happy to have her back, and we had sisterly conversations into the night, lying on the bed together. Luckily I could speak Japanese, but I remember correcting her English pronunciation. (Perhaps I should not be harsh on the Japanese, as here in Canada non-speakers pronounce Japanese words without much care; for example, *karaoke* has turned into *carry-oki*.)

Though I was a bit nervous about going to Vancouver, a place I had little memory of, I had full confidence in my ability to welcome my sister home on my own. This reflects the upbringing I had had to this point, having always looked after my siblings.

I believe Kikuko had a difficult time upon returning in adjusting to both our family and to Canadian culture. I recall, upon our arrival in Winnipeg, the looks of discomfort (not welcome) her younger brothers offered her. They had been expecting an older sister to rejoin our family, but I believe the fact that Kikuko could not speak English adequately made her a stranger to them. Here, I blame Mother. Why had she not prepared our younger siblings for this first meeting with their sister? But then, Mother had not prepared herself. She mentions in her memoir her shock at greeting an adult daughter at the train station, not the child she remembered and had longed for.

Luckily, at this time there were other Kika Nisei returned to Canada, several to Winnipeg families. (Kika Nisei refers to those who, though born in Canada, were sent to Japan for a visit or to be educated and did not return until the war ended and restrictions were finally lifted.) A couple of young women (the two Matsubara sisters) and a few of the young men became Kikuko's close friends. I have memories of joining this group whenever they made a weekend trip during the summertime to Grand Beach, tenting on the sand. Some evenings, after my parents had purchased and moved into our new home on Beverley Street, I joined them in singing Japanese songs in our living room. Those are happy memories.

I often wonder if my sister might have had a more satisfying life had she remained in Japan. I am told by relatives and friends who grew up with her in Japan that she was an excellent student and had ambition to continue into further studies. Even in the aftermath of the war, Grandmother would have been well able to afford my sister's education.

Grandmother was known as an intelligent and well-educated woman, someone who might have been called a feminist if that had been possible in the Japan of that time. She travelled extensively as an agent recruiting nurses, even while her granddaughter was living with her. As Nēchan told us, whenever Obāchan (Grandma) was away, which was regularly on such business trips, she would move next door to stay with her cousins, Uncle Konosuke's family.

Kikuko was soon to be called Kay, just as I had turned from Eiko to Grace. Her immediate focus was on improving her English but also on finding work, since she was expected to contribute to the family. So, after registering at English-language classes, she began to take a course in hairdressing, suggested to her by friends as an easier occupation to pursue with limited English. While returning to Canada may have fulfilled my sister's wish to reunite with family members (her letters of yearning to return had regularly been received by Mother), our parents were, sad to say, at this time not sympathetic parents, having little time for us, working hard each day to put food on the table for a family of six, now seven, soon to be joined also by a nephew from Japan.

Kikuko had had a protected life surrounded by relatives in Mio, where wartime suffering was not as great as in many other areas (particularly cities) in Japan. Because the family owned property, she had not experienced undue poverty, but I recall her telling me stories of the hardships faced by many village folks and of children coming to the door at mealtime to await leftovers. Sweet potatoes had become the staple in those days instead of rice, which was scarce.

Although there was certainly no sign of a welcome mat when we first moved to Winnipeg, there soon developed a lot of interest (or curiosity, perhaps) in Japanese Canadians, or whatever it was we represented to people at that time. Through Miss Blanche Megaffin, a retired missionary who had once worked in Japan, I was introduced to Knox United Church. The Japanese Canadian Christian community, hiring a Japanese-speaking minister of their own, soon began Sunday services there. I joined the main church choir and also the Young People's Union, and I participated in a musical play, Gilbert and Sullivan's operetta *The Mikado*. I remember practising my part, singing "Three Little Maids from School Are We."

The Manitoba Japanese Canadian Citizens' Association began to sponsor annual concerts called *shibai*, usually held at the Ukrainian Labour Temple hall. Some experienced senior members, the Issei, and older members of the second-generation Nisei, both men and women, invited younger members of the community to participate. I was one of the younger ones, learning the Japanese traditional *odori* (dance) taught particularly by our family friend Mrs. Asako Oye, who played the *shamisen*, a Japanese string instrument, and sang, while my sister and I and a friend, Chizu Nakata, danced. I also began singing popular Japanese songs onstage before a large crowd, taught to me by my sister Kay, who kept up with current trends through her continuing contact with friends in Japan.

I recall one song related to postwar Japan titled "Kankan Musume," the slang name for women encouraged or recruited by the government to entertain American occupation soldiers. I have since learned that such songs were making reference not to prostitutes but to daughters of postwar families sent to the city from poverty-stricken villages. As women, they had little choice but to serve their country in this way, just as the men had served without much choice during the war years. Regrettably, I learned to sing such songs without comprehending the context.

As we settled into city life, we Japanese Canadian young women found ourselves invited to social events and were often asked to wear Japanese kimonos, even though most of us had never worn one until such interest arose. I believe we were, in those days, looked upon as exotic creatures. But we accepted these as welcoming gestures.

Many young Nisei men, with cameras once again in hand (cameras had been confiscated in 1942), were now eager to engage in photography and looked to us girls to satisfy their creative curiosities about traditions forgotten or never known, depending on their ages. Young women were invited to pose wearing beautiful kimonos sent by grandmothers in Japan, as was the case with my older sister and me, or brought to Canada more recently by Kika Nisei or new immigrants.

There were also many events at which media, including the CBC and the Winnipeg newspapers (the *Free Press* and the *Tribune*), requested Japanese Canadians, usually young women, to pose or be interviewed, often together with young women representing other ethnic communities, for example, Chinese or Ukrainian.

A few years later, while volunteering as a member of the Manitoba Japanese Canadian Citizens' Association, and soon to be its first female president, I was introduced to the Japanese consul general, Mr. Norihiko Kikkawa, and his family. He and his wife and their young daughter often invited me to their home, once even to a dinner attended by Ambassador Koto Matsudaira, who served as an ambassador to the United Nations from 1957 to 1961. When I met him, he was on his way to this post in New York.

When the consul general's office received a request from the local Hudson's Bay Company store for someone to model an outfit described (exotically) with Japanese labels such as *kabuki* and *obi* (sash) attached, I was recommended. I appeared in a full-length ad in the *Winnipeg Tribune* on April 16, 1959. It was an interesting period, a learning experience for me.

ᏭᎤ

Looking back, I recall and now question the content of the compositions I handed in to my high school English teacher, Miss Christie, at St. John's Technical High School shortly after we had moved to Winnipeg. I was in grade ten. When we were told to write about our everyday lives, the subjects I chose made reference to the life I was leading at that moment with my family, one totally foreign to my fellow classmates and undoubtedly boring. I don't remember ever writing about the internment years or being asked to speak about them. But Miss Christie took to reading my compositions aloud in class. I thought it was because they were good and felt complimented, but today I wonder. Was her interest more in the exotic, about a Japanese Canadian family recently freed from internment restrictions, living a life perhaps abnormal to her and to my classmates, though normal to me?

Grace, posing in a kimono for one of the many events held to draw media attention to Winnipeg's growing Japanese Canadian population, in an effort to showcase the city's multiculturalism. Author's personal collection.

I was living in a city for the first time since childhood. But as a teenager, I spent my weekdays once again ensuring the safety of my baby sister (now school-aged) and my younger brothers as they returned daily from their respective schools after I had bicycled home from high school, then starting dinner before Mother returned from her job at the

garment factory. My weekends were spent largely with Mother, laundering, ironing, washing floors and staircases (particularly in the part of our
house that was rented to others) and grocery shopping. There was little
time left for homework or for developing friendships or engaging in any
social activities, but I did enjoy school, particularly my English classes.

During this period, young students, largely men, were arriving
from Ontario and Quebec to attend the University of Manitoba, in
particular the Engineering and Architecture Departments. They came
from families whose parents had already been well established in Canada before the war and had opted to settle in the East in 1942 (rather
than going to the restricted BC internment sites), so they were able to
afford to continue their children's education soon after restrictions were
lifted. While the University of British Columbia had expelled Japanese
Canadian students soon after the war was declared, the University of
Manitoba had opened its doors to a few Japanese Canadian students
even in 1942. It was also one of the first Canadian universities to accept
such students after 1949.

Most importantly, I was for the first time being introduced to the
idea of a university education, even though it was not yet within my
reach. Up to this time the word *university* had had no resonance for
me. It was unaffordable, never discussed as an option. But now it was
something that possibly could include me, perhaps in the near future.

However, when I look back to this period, I recall my insecurity. I
was still not sure who I was. Most of my Japanese Canadian girlfriends
had older sisters or brothers (or had Nisei parents), and they seemed
confidently focused on their everyday lives, accepting themselves without question as fellow Canadians. Most had forgotten Japanese language
and customs, conversing with one another in English, while I was still
depending on Mother, and she on me. I was still expecting we would
one day be moving again, perhaps returning to the West Coast. That
was a topic of conversation among many community members who had
settled in Winnipeg, and several of our Kika Nisei relatives had already
returned to Vancouver or to Steveston.

I accepted racialized life as the norm, since that was how my life
had been to date. Many of the people I had met in Whitemouth, and

now in Winnipeg, were friendly and supportive. Some of the young people I met at school made an active effort to become friends. Yet nothing to date had been lasting or permanent. Soon after making new friends, I was always moving to another location, and I never looked back as I confronted new challenges.

I realize now that I did not take time to appreciate the meaning of friendship. My life was not something I felt I could discuss or argue about and have understood by others, except by Mother, in the kitchen. I didn't recognize that friendship was not only about social life but also something that could be personal and made deeper through sharing. I was living in limbo, just as I believe my parents had been doing before moving to Winnipeg.

I had, up to that point, attempted to avoid contact with the word *Jap* by smiling a lot and being nice to those around me in order to receive friendly responses. I hadn't yet thought about how to counteract discriminatory behaviour by others, except through avoidance. Although I had by this time learned to argue with Mother and to take stubborn stances on some issues, outside of home I was timid.

One day in the early 1950s, I made a major discovery. On a late Saturday afternoon, I was as usual walking the aisles of the William Avenue public library, looking for something new and interesting to read. In those days, I was not yet aware of book reviews and did not know anyone who could recommend books to me, but my favourite pastime was reading novels. In fact, Russian novels. I don't remember who had introduced them to me. Could it have been my high school English teacher? In any case, my favourite pastimes were those spent in solitude, reading. (Perhaps this is true even today.)

On this day, I was stopped by a title on one shelf that included the words *Japanese Canadian*. I thought to myself, Who in the world would be interested in writing about us? Such was my ignorance at that time.

The book I discovered that Saturday afternoon was *The Canadian Japanese and World War II: A Sociological and Psychological Account*, by sociologist Forrest E. La Violette, published in 1948. As I would learn, it was the first book to describe the social and psychological effects of the 1942 uprooting of people of Japanese ancestry from Canada's West

Coast. Reading it would bring me to the realization that while I had been living in discomfort in Canada, the only country I knew, in the obviously unacceptable skin that I had inherited, I had never seriously questioned what had happened to us as Japanese Canadians or delved into our history. I believed simply that the uprooting from our homes on the West Coast had to do with Canada's declaration of war on Japan. Without franchise, we were treated as "enemy aliens." But the question remained: How was it that we had not been released at the end of the war, not been allowed to return to our homes? I had not yet connected the dots regarding the racism promoted by all levels of government that explained why we alone had been interned.

I thumbed through the pages of La Violette's book, first in a corner of the library where I could remain hidden as though I were doing something illegal. Then, instead of borrowing a novel as usual, I took this book home.

It was a revelation. Even as a child, living in one of the interior sites of British Columbia, I had been aware, through listening to whispered conversations between my parents and their friends, that these were years of stress and that people were worried about what the future would hold.

Later, I had overheard people discuss with one another the hardship years and the subsequent decision forced upon each of them when the "dispersal" order was issued.

Now, their focus was entirely on moving ahead, not an easy task, but at least they could make their own decision based on their needs and abilities. In meeting one another for the first time in their new post-1950 lives, the first question people asked was "Where were you and your family, which internment camp?" The question was no longer "Which prefecture in Japan do you come from?" the pre-1942 question they had posed one another with interest as immigrants.

After reading La Violette's book, I wrote and submitted two articles to the Manitoba Japanese Canadian Citizens' Association's monthly newsletter, *The Outlook*, to share with my friends and community my excitement at discovering a history I had lived through as a child without awareness. My book review must have seemed ridiculously outdated to the readers, most of whom were settled in to their new lives in this city, living without the need to look back to those years. Likely much of it was plagiarized, since I didn't have a clue yet about writing articles for publication. For whatever reason, the editor kindly printed them.

Not long afterwards, I bumped into Dr. Victor Shimizu, dean of philosophy at United College (now the University of Winnipeg). He very kindly said he had read my articles and offered me praise. I can today imagine that, while he might have found my articles amusing in their innocence, as an educated man, a scholar, also of Japanese heritage, he was pleased a young person had taken interest in her history and wanted to share her discoveries. That is how I feel today as more and more young Asian Canadians seek out information about their own family histories, the daily struggles of facing and overcoming racial injustice.

⋘

With my parents focused on resettlement, especially with my younger siblings still in public school, I decided to attend a business college, adding to the skills I had already acquired in high school. In those days, high school was split into commercial and academic courses to prepare students for their choice of career. I picked up basic skills in typing and shorthand toward a career as a stenographer, and then took evening classes at Success Business College to earn a certificate.

Within a year, when I was not yet eighteen, I began working at British North America Insurance Company, where I was accepted with generosity and kindness by the manager, the agent and staff members. I can still recall the friendly faces. I was the only non-white person employed by the firm, and I believe that for most of them it was their first experience working with a Japanese or Asian Canadian person. I was invited to staff socials and activities, which helped me to develop enough confidence in my abilities to start looking to the larger world of opportunities.

Upon hearing of the Anthes-Imperial Company, a cast iron pipe foundry that had hired a number of resettled Japanese Canadian men, and seeing the factory's advertisement for a stenographer in the local newspaper, I applied and was hired. Here, too, everyone welcomed me.

Since the company was located on the outskirts of the city, a member of the staff kindly picked me up and took me home each day. Any fears I had had of feeling like an outsider quickly disappeared, even as I worked hard to understand and fit into Western culture.

Within a year, the secretary to the vice-president left and I was invited to become the boss's secretary. It was a major step forward for me.

Learning of my promotion, the Japanese Canadian men working in the foundry, who were already proud of me simply for working in this office, gave me big smiles whenever I saw them in the cafeteria. I was proud of them, too. Our lives were changing drastically. We were all originally British Columbians, uprooted from our homes, and were now finally fully accepted as Canadians, at least here in this foundry. We were each of us, old and young, establishing ourselves in this new environment as best we could with support not only from one another but also from a large segment of Winnipeg's various communities.

It was here, at the Anthes-Imperial Company, that my life took a turn. Not only was I accepted in the office by my co-workers, both plant management and the office staff, but my social relationships with them were normal even outside of the office. Professionals such as the engineers who visited from the company's head office in St. Catharines all made me feel that I belonged. I had become one of them.

Having been raised by a mother who always took pains to dress me well, I paid attention during this period to what others wore. Most women were wearing casual clothes, while I was always dressed as though I were going to a business meeting. As my self-confidence grew, I soon became more casual in appearance, too.

My boss, Mr. David Russell, aware of my history and seeing how socially naive I was, helped me to gain confidence by introducing me to various aspects of Canadian culture. He and his wife kindly began inviting me to join them at Winnipeg Blue Bombers games and even Winnipeg Symphony Orchestra concerts, invitations that I accepted with wide eyes. This was my first exposure to such social and cultural activities. I had a lot to learn.

I recall one instance of my cultural ignorance. When Mr. Russell, while dictating a letter, used the idiom *not my cup of tea*, I questioned whether I had heard right. I had no idea what he was talking about. There were, of course, many other instances, but he always took time to patiently explain things to me.

Mr. Russell became my adviser on many fronts. Even after he relocated a couple of years later to the head office in Ontario, he kindly kept in touch with me. When I decided to move to Vancouver in 1957, he contacted his business friends and arranged a temporary job for me in the steno pool at BC Electric on Burrard Street. Whenever he came on business trips to Vancouver during the almost two years I spent there, he always contacted me to make sure I was okay.

In the meantime, my parents were contending with their own problems.

FATHER'S ILLNESS AND RECOVERY

Mother:

My husband had for many years complained about his stomach. He was finally diagnosed as suffering from a duodenal ulcer and underwent surgery. The doctor, I.M. Grant, assured me that even if there was cancer, it had all been removed so there was nothing to worry about.

After his discharge from hospital, his diet had to be soft food in limited amounts. At the hospital, he had wished to eat more, but when he was given extra, he threw it up. This was repeated several times until he got used to the new diet, and for the next two years during recuperation, he enrolled in a cooking school and found employment at the Marlborough Hotel as a cook's assistant.

During the time my husband was recuperating, our two daughters and then our older son began working, so they helped in supporting and maintaining the household.

Father had always enjoyed cooking, perhaps due to his early experience of working in the dining room of the hotel in Winnipeg. For this reason, in our household it was normal to have *yōshoku* (Western food), and breakfast was always porridge (which I hated) for the kids, followed by toast and jam, usually marmalade (Father's choice). Mother occasionally took me to a local Safeway to buy peanut butter, a rare treat. I recall on Sunday mornings waking up to the smell of pancakes, which Father would make for us.

On celebratory occasions, Mother usually prepared traditional maki sushi and sashimi, with various dishes cooked in the Japanese style, such as tempura or sukiyaki. But the Sunday family menu in our home pre-1942 was rare roast beef with grated horseradish, gravy and mashed or baked potatoes, as well as a dessert such as tapioca pudding or the pound cake Mother soon learned to bake, all Father's choices. The menu was more British, I suppose, than Canadian, but then Canada was a British Commonwealth country.

Most immigrant families we knew ate from a Japanese menu even for breakfast—rice and green tea, pickles and fish—until their Nisei children began contributing to the makeup of a Western menu.

As Mother writes in her memoir, Father found work first in the kitchen at the Marlborough Hotel; he then worked at Misericordia Hospital, where my sister Keiko had begun training to become a registered nurse. I think these, his last work years, were happier times for him.

Mother continues:

In around 1951 or 1952, Nishikihama Konosuke's fourth daughter in Japan became ill with an inner ear problem, producing a high fever that could not be controlled. Left like this, she would die, and even if she should recover, she might already have suffered permanent brain damage. The family was told that if they could get hold of some penicillin, she could be healed, but in the Japan of that time, such medicinal help as penicillin could not be accessed. The emergency message came to us to send the penicillin immediately.

We went to consult with the Manitoba Buddhist church minister, Rev. Nishimura, and through him accessed a doctor and were able to send the penicillin to Japan. Since this was done through the Red Cross, as a matter of emergency, the medication was sent directly to a doctor in the town of Gobo [not far from Mio]. As a result, our niece recovered, and today she is the mother of three children. I feel very grateful to Rev. Nishimura for the assistance he gave us in this regard.

From about 1954 on, those who had returned to Japan before and after the war began returning to Canada, including the daughter of my husband's brother Taguchi Katsutaro and three sons and a married daughter of his other brother, Nishikihama Konosuke.

We received word at this time from Konosuke-niisan that he wanted to send his fourth son, Hiroaki, to Canada to study English, and he suggested his son attend school from our home.

Since the end of the war, in order to begin our lives all over again, we were barely making ends meet, and I felt he had nerve to ask. Everyone knew the conditions in which Japanese Canadians were living at this time. I remembered that I had not received any money from him for board in Minto, when we were living in the house that was pulled into the town site, paying rent of $570 a year.

We had done everything in accordance with Niisan's wishes since leaving Vancouver. With regard to ordering fish from the fish market in Vancouver, I am not aware who paid for the costs. But in Vernon, when my husband and his brother met, excluding me from the meeting, the brother had calculated that $300 was owed to him. This is what my husband told me when we arrived in Winnipeg. There was nothing in writing, no questions asked, so on each payday, with great effort, I made up parcels and sent them to Japan.

In Japan, the brother was selling everything we sent through the black market, and since there was a shortage of sugar, he requested that we send saccharine. At that time one pound of saccharine was quite costly even in Canada. For fear of customs inspection and discovery, which would mean that it would be disposed of, I had at one time taken the precaution of putting a pound of saccharine in the bottom of a cocoa tin, then filling it to the top with cocoa powder. But when the tin arrived in Japan, not taking care to read my instructions, they sold the cocoa. I was very upset over this.

In this way, the $300 debt was totally paid off.

Having five children of our own, we had good reason to turn him down, but we decided one more at the table wouldn't make such a huge difference and decided to accept the son into our family.

During and after the war, Hiroaki [who was soon re-named Jerry by his new friends] had not studied English, but he entered junior high here in Canada. Although he could manage other subjects, he knew little English, and so Eiko, after speaking to someone from his class, daily reviewed with him what he had learned. It was quite a feat. Then he had an attack of appendicitis and had to undergo surgery. Every day before I went to work and again when I returned home, I boiled water and cleaned the surgery wound, applying a poultice, until it was at last healed.

Then, having completed two years of schooling in June, Hiroaki was introduced by someone we knew to a signboard company and got a job drawing. So, around Christmas time, I suggested that now that he was working, he might contribute toward his board. But he said he could not afford it as he had to send money to his parents. So this was left as it was, and he continued to receive free board. (I have often thought to myself that sometimes being good-hearted might be related to being a fool.)

The following year, since his parents came from Japan to live in Vancouver with their other sons and daughter, I sent him back to them.

While he was living with us, Hiroaki learned the chick-sexing trade from his cousin, Taguchi Yoshiyo. Hiroaki's father had written to Yoshiyo to ask him to teach this trade to his son. Hiroaki had first returned to BC but then went to Toronto, to his cousin's, and depended on him for a job and training and began working in Toronto as a chick sexer. He in time married someone distantly related to his mother.

I can understand Mother's feelings of reluctance at being asked to accept another child at our table. She was working long hours every day, as was Father, to maintain a household of three children still in public school and to pay off the mortgage on the house they had just purchased and had moved into only recently. There is no doubt that she felt this brother-in-law had taken advantage of her husband during the years he was living here in Canada. As the younger brother, Father had little choice but to comply with the older brother's wishes.

In recalling this experience in her memoir, Mother reveals the disappointment she felt that this nephew, after moving away and later getting married, never once acknowledged the special effort our family had made on his behalf, especially at a time when we were struggling to establish a new life with both parents working, in a new environment. Undoubtedly, he alone was not to be blamed. Not only was he young and naive, but also, as the youngest member of his family of eight siblings, he was used to everyone looking out for him. He had no appreciation of the hardships endured by Japanese Canadian families, even his own, during those years. I think his father should have been the one to show appreciation, but my father, being the younger brother, was not offered any thanks. I remember Mother always feeling that Father was kind to a fault.

UNIONS AND REUNIONS

Mother:

In June 1958, our oldest daughter's wedding reception was held at the Marlborough Hotel. My second daughter had found work in a company where a number of Japanese Canadian men were hired, the Anthes-Imperial Co. Ltd. She met and married a co-worker in May 1959.

My husband moved to a cooking job at Misericordia Hospital, where, in the meantime, our youngest daughter had begun training as a registered nurse after high school. She graduated in 1963, married and continued to work at this hospital.

I decided in 1961 to visit my mother-in-law to see how she was and began to make arrangements to go to Japan for the first time since the end of the war. The planes were flying by this time, so I contacted Iwata Travel in Vancouver, and Iwata Kenichi-san sent me the tickets by mail and introduced me to others who were going at the same time.

At this time, the Vancouver–Haneda airfare was $888, and while those who went with me continued on with their trip upon arrival in Japan, I stayed overnight at an inn, the Yuhonya, and departed early the next morning for Kobe by train. When I arrived at the station, my sister and her husband were there to greet me. For the first time in thirty years, I had returned to Mio.

Thirty years' time had taken its toll on my mother-in-law, now seventy-seven years of age. Just like the *kotowaza* [proverb] says, "Ten years, one era." I saw the people in my home village as the epitome of humanity and ephemerality:

Saigetsu hito wo matazu [Time waits for no one].

Each tree I had observed as a child, each blade of grass, everything held a feeling of yearning, and I met those I had gone to school with with nostalgia.

My mother-in-law took advantage of my visit and hired Oye-san to remove the second floor of her home to make it into a one-storey house, for better ventilation.

My older sister, Mori Yoshiko, who had returned to Japan from Canada in 1935 with a family of three children, and my younger sister, Suzuko Hideyo, were there, and we had a reunion.

Mother, as I recall, returned to Japan only three times throughout her life in Canada. She had come from Japan as Father's bride at the end of 1929, at the age of only eighteen. Her first trip back in 1961 was to ensure that Grandmother, her mother-in-law, was well, as is the duty of a daughter-in-law. My parents had lost full contact with Japan between 1942 and 1949, since letters were censored in those days, and things returned to normal only after the return of their first daughter from Japan.

After contributing to the family income for a few years, I took time off and moved to Vancouver in 1957. I needed some distance to deal with issues around the man that I was considering marrying, who was of Scottish heritage.

Mixed marriages, though they became the norm soon after, took a while in those days to be absorbed by parents. While the concept has been around for centuries, it was known to most at the time mainly through romantic and fictional stories, such as *Madama Butterfly*, the opera by Giacomo Puccini. Of course such stories of colonial times did not have happy endings for the colonized. When I was growing up, parents in general, not only Japanese Canadian parents, were not open to their children dating someone from another culture or intermarrying.

My parents, however, accepted the man who would become my husband. They knew I had met Al (Alistair) at Anthes-Imperial, where he was working as a draftsman, and that he was at that time an engineering student. They accepted him almost from the moment they met him. I sometimes wonder if Father, having come to Canada at the young age of nineteen, had observed cross-cultural relationships and so was able to look at the larger picture when considering my so-called "mixed" marriage. His close friend, Harry Sasaki, had married a British woman as early as the 1920s in Winnipeg. Interestingly, Mother, though not fluent in English, was very open while Al and I were dating, and he was always welcome in our home. This behaviour was rare among parents in those days.

At that time, arranged marriages were still common. Parents would choose a marriage partner for their son or daughter after careful investigation into the other family's roots. In fact, during my late teens, my parents had at least three proposals of marriage for me. I recall I was not even asked my opinion. Mother received the offers and turned them down on my behalf; thank goodness!

Usually proposals like this came through family friends or relatives. However, I had one interesting proposal from a relative stranger, a young man from a distinguished family in Japan whom I had met during his visit to Winnipeg. He had come as a journalist, affiliated with a major newspaper in Tokyo. More importantly, he had come as the English-language interpreter for a cousin of the Japanese emperor who had lost his title with the American occupation after the Second World War. The former prince, Mr. Tsuneyoshi Takeda, heading up the Skating Union of Japan, brought a Japanese hockey team to play against an Ontario team, the Kenora Thistles, in the mid-1950s and stayed in Winnipeg during his visit.

Even though I was young, I had been elected the first female president of the Manitoba Japanese Canadian Citizens' Association in 1955. In this role, together with members of the Japanese Canadian community of Winnipeg, I had welcomed Mr. Takeda's party with a community banquet. Several private parties were also held by local Japanese Canadian families and business people.

There was much publicity in the local media around this visit, considering Mr. Takeda's status. After the team had finished their tour and returned to Japan, I received a very kind thank-you letter signed by both Mr. Takeda and his interpreter, Mr. H, for the welcome we had offered them and the team. Mr. H continued contact with me off and on, sending letters and a holiday greeting. I was too naive (or just too careless) to realize that he was interested in me personally, even after he had asked for a photo and wondered if I would not be interested in working in Japan, perhaps for the airline, and said he could arrange this for me.

A year or so later, when I was living in Vancouver, a relative told me she had heard from Mother that there had been a marriage proposal for me. I immediately telephoned Mother, who promptly informed me that, yes, there had been a proposal from someone representing Mr. H, but that she had *hakkiri to kotowatta* (very clearly turned it down). And so that was that. Mother was not going to let me marry a foreigner, but she approved of a Scottish Canadian!

While in Vancouver, I worked in the BC Electric steno pool, the job arranged for me by Mr. Russell. I met a few young people from the Japanese Canadian community through a childhood friend, Michiko Motomochi, who was one of my classmates at the Japanese Language School prior to 1942. Her mother, Mrs. Motomochi, had been my teacher. I made some new and interesting friends, even dating one medical student briefly, which led me to wonder and consider if I should remain in Vancouver. I was enjoying my stay in the city, attending various functions and even joining the choir of the Japanese Canadian United Church.

I had responded to a newspaper ad for a live-in babysitter and was soon living with a young Jewish couple with two little sons. I was lucky to receive free room and board, babysitting on evenings and weekends as required, while working at a daytime job. The couple were very interesting and also very kind. It was a great experience for me to learn about another culture, including the food, which I enjoyed watching them cook, especially my favourite, knishes, with roast chicken. We lived quite close to Queen Elizabeth Park, so I took the little boys for walks there.

I returned home to Winnipeg in June 1958 to attend my sister Kikuko's wedding, at which time Al and I made our final decision and became engaged. I find it incredible in retrospect that my in-laws did not oppose our marriage, considering it had been only ten years since

Japanese Canadians had been released and offered Canadian citizen-ship. (It is noteworthy that my father-in-law was a high-ranking mili-tary man, an Officer of the Order of the British Empire. I remember him as a very kind father-in-law and a loving grandfather to our two sons.)

And so, with the parents on both sides giving us their blessings, we had a beautiful marriage ceremony at Knox United Church on May 16, 1959, to which our friends and relatives were invited. They joined us at the reception afterwards at the Marion Hotel in St. Boniface. Mother, together with my already married older sister and a few friends, made a huge batch of shrimp tempura and some sushi to serve at the wedding reception. It was a custom among Japanese Canadian families in those days in Winnipeg to serve such food after the Western-style wedding dinner, as the evening of music and dancing progressed.

After an hour or more of dancing, we left the reception to change into our honeymoon clothes, then returned to say goodbye, me throw-ing my bouquet to my single friends. Needless to say, Mother had made both my beautiful wedding gown and my honeymoon travel suit. We spent our honeymoon in Milwaukee, going to Chicago to a baseball game, and then touring the Dells in Wisconsin. It was my first visit to the United States.

Mr. and Mrs. David Russell sent us a wedding gift from St. Cath-arines. Later, on one of his business trips to Winnipeg, he took time to visit when our first son, Michael, was born. Sadly, not too long after, an office staff member phoned to let me know that Mr. Russell had passed away during emergency brain surgery. It was a great shock to me. Mem-ories of him remain with me as someone very dear who contributed greatly to who I was able to become, a woman confident enough to be-gin pursuing her own direction into the future. I wish today that I could more properly have acknowledged and thanked him.

It was not until I was married to an educated person with educat-ed friends, all from middle-to-upper-class families living in and around Winnipeg's River Heights, that my need to understand who I was began to resurface.

The life I had chosen as my own, and soon with two sons, was the kind of privileged life I had watched from the outside and desired

Grace married Alistair Thomson in May of 1959. Despite the prospect of an arranged marriage to a Japanese man, Grace's mother promptly turned it down on
her daughter's behalf and welcomed Alistair, who was of Scottish ancestry, into
the family. Author's personal collection

without cultural understanding. I found myself living a role I had created for myself—that of a white woman, in a white household, doing all
those things I had heretofore seen only in white magazines and movies.
Except that I was not white and never could be.

   Not all of us living at the margins of Canadian society are unhap-
py to be there, though we may not be comfortable. We are, in fact, occupying diverse and often interesting spaces, accepted or not. I believe
now that it is only through recognizing the existence of such margins
that the authority of the centre can be maintained. In intermarrying,
I was occupying the margins and the centre simultaneously, but I had
not yet realized this.

This telling of my story is, I think, a therapeutic act, moving toward resolution of a past that I had always held in abeyance as insoluble. For a long time I put the blame on my immigrant mother for not offering me proper mothering. I was always given the role of looking after my siblings, which did not leave much space or time to experience the outside social environment, but I know now that there is no "proper" mothering, since there is no "proper" world. We all have to make sense of our own lives and accept some fragmentations as natural, like a jigsaw puzzle with a piece missing. Mother, too, lived with a piece missing, but before she passed, I believe she found peace through her Buddhist faith.

After my second son was born, I began once again to think about identity issues, which led me to contemplate university education. Such thoughts were precipitated by my awareness that my sons, though still young, were beginning to notice their mother's obvious difference through the eyes of their friends.

When my younger son was about five years old, he returned home perplexed after playing with a neighbourhood boy who was slightly older, saying his friend Brucie had told him that he was Chinese and put his fingers on his face to slant his eyes. How should a mother respond, especially when this was a rerun of something experienced in her own life? I did my best, explaining that it was not about being Chinese (or Asian), that each of us was different. Brucie had carrot hair and blue eyes. The important thing was that we liked one another, were friends—that such differences were to be appreciated. How else could I have explained it to a preschool child? I was not prepared for this. Undoubtedly, Brucie, not yet in grade school, had been informed by his parents as to what his friend, my son, was (Chinese). He had not come to such a conclusion on his own.

YEARS OF SORROW

In 1963, my parents decided to move back to the West Coast, where they had begun their married life. Mother writes:

> We had become seniors, but in Winnipeg the people who gathered together as members of the Jōdo Shinshū sect were all very warm and kind, and like family to us. While we worked hard after the war for some seventeen years in Manitoba, our children were getting married and we were now blessed with grandchildren. However, in view of the severity of the cold weather that had no end, we decided to move back to the gentler climate of British Columbia, and so we put our house up for sale. With a farewell party given us by the Buddhist church, and receiving various generous gifts, we departed in tears on August 16, 1963. We boarded a train and headed for Vancouver. We left the sale of the Winnipeg house to our daughter Eiko and decided to spend the rest of our lives in Vancouver.
>
> We had lived in the prairie province for a long time, so as we approached Vancouver, we felt great nostalgia in seeing once again the mountains and the sea. Whether it was the smell of the seashore or the fragrance of the sea, it was like returning to one's *furusato*, one's home village—North Vancouver's mountains, the seabus, the ships from all over the world carrying freight, the tourist cruise ships coming and going, the ebb and flow of the tide. The haze hanging on the mountains and the fog turning into snow: spring, summer, autumn and winter, I enjoyed the million-dollar parade of scenic landscapes passing before my eyes.

The years passed quickly and soon it was spring again, and before I knew it, I had turned eighty-six years of age, writing my life.

In returning to Vancouver, my parents found not the vibrant Paueru Gai they had left in 1942 but an abandoned neighbourhood, now referred to as "skid row" by outsiders. And so they moved into an apartment on Victoria Drive. I believe, though, that they felt settled back in the place where they had begun their lives together, where they belonged.

Mother and Father participated in the 1977 Japanese Canadian Centennial *sakura* (cherry tree) planting ceremony at Oppenheimer Park. The planting ceremony was, I think, an act of loyalty, marking a remembered connection to this place. By planting cherry trees during this celebration of the hundred-year anniversary of the first Japanese immigrant to come to Canada, my parents and other seniors were reclaiming their history, owning their history, while not forgetting their struggles, their pain, their longing for this place, remembered as their *furusato*, their home away from home, a safe place, especially during the internment years. They were joined by young descendants and new immigrants who felt the passion and yearnings of the elders as they heard stories about this place and the not-too-distant past.

Undoubtedly, this period of resettlement on the West Coast was the beginning of the process that eventually moved toward the Japanese Canadian Redress campaign of the 1980s.

When my parents made the choice to return to Vancouver, it was not just about the place where they had begun their married life, or about the climate. I believe it was also important for them to catch up to their two sons, who had left Winnipeg earlier to fulfill their own dreams.

When he was in his teens, the younger of my two brothers, Kenji, was caught breaking into a warehouse with a friend. After a trial at which he was represented by a distinguished lawyer (for whom I was working as a secretary at the time), he was released by the judge, who I believe saw the predicament in which my parents were living sympathetically and offered my brother a chance to begin a new life. He subsequently moved to the West Coast, where some of his older Kika Nisei cousins had settled.

Upon returning to Vancouver, Sawae and her husband participated in the sakura planting ceremony at Oppenheimer Park in 1977, a centennial celebration of the first Japanese immigrant to arrive in Canada. Photo by Tamio Wakayama, courtesy of Mayumi Takasaki

He never kept this part of his life a secret, sharing the story with his young friends and relatives while living his life to the fullest, and was soon operating a dry-cleaning shop of his own in Vancouver. When he died in 2001 at age sixty-two, he was remembered by his friends as a kind and generous man. Many people attended his memorial gathering, even some old friends from Winnipeg, who shared personal and often funny stories of experiences with him. He was indeed loved by many.

The older of my two brothers, Toyoaki (Tom), after graduating high school and helping our parents with the mortgage payments for a year, moved to the West Coast and got himself a job at a logging camp in Port Alberni. In the letters I received from him, he wrote about topping trees and playing baseball with his workmates. Tall, athletic and artistically talented, he showed great promise. Within a year or so, with the money he had saved, he moved to Vancouver and started attending the British Columbia Institute of Technology (BCIT), where he trained as an arc welder. After several years of working locally, including as part of the crew that built the Second Narrows Bridge, and internationally, building oil tanks in Indonesia for Bechtel Corporation, he was back at BCIT, this time as an instructor. However, Tom had problems. He was carrying a lot of frustration, perhaps even buried anger, from the past. He died at the young age of forty-seven.

৩৯

The years between 1983 and 1986 were years of sorrow in our lives, as Mother describes:

> My elder son's wife, Marilyn, died in July; then my son Toyoaki himself passed away from this world in October 1983, leaving his one dear son behind. Then, in February 1985, my husband, who had never caught a cold in his life, died of lung cancer, and in March of the following year, my first daughter, who lived in Winnipeg, passed. I was at a loss to explain to myself what was happening to our lives. When I came to my senses, I realized I was still alive.

Mother's two remaining daughters, Keiko and me, were both living in Winnipeg with our own families, each of us travelling back and forth to Vancouver during this time.

My dear older sister, Kikuko, died of lung cancer at the young age of fifty-five, leaving behind her beloved husband and three children, two sons and a daughter, barely into their adulthood. There is no doubt that during her relatively short life in Canada, she contributed to our community in various ways. She taught Japanese at the Manitoba Buddhist Temple hall for many years. She also led efforts to establish a sister-city affiliation between Fort Garry, the suburb of Winnipeg where she resided with her family, and Setagaya City in Japan.

When I visited Japan years later in 2016, I was invited by a group of Japanese scholars headed by Dr. Masako Iino in Tokyo to offer stories of the experiences of Kika Nisei. In my presentation, I used my sister's experience as an example. I was surprised to learn that one of the participants remembered my sister's name, Kikuko (Nishikihama) Tazumi, as being included in documents filed in Setagaya City about the sister-city affiliation with the City of Winnipeg (Municipality of Fort Garry). I was happy to learn this, to know that a part of my sister remains, appreciated, in Japan, where she had spent her school years into adulthood.

The 1980s were when Japanese Canadians now living scattered across Canada, led by the National Association of Japanese Canadians, campaigned toward achieving redress from the Government of Canada. On September 22, 1988, Prime Minister Brian Mulroney issued an apology for the "miscarriage of justice." The Japanese Canadian Redress Agreement was signed by both the prime minister and the president of the National Association of Japanese Canadians, Art Miki. The token redress payment of $21,000 to each survivor could hardly compensate for the lost years, property losses and family disruptions and separations.

The psychological scars and memories of injustice remain with many of us even to this day.

Friends often ask me what role I played during the redress campaign. Sadly, during this decade, our family was arranging and attending one funeral after another: my dear sister-in-law Marilyn, my brother Toyoaki, my father and my sister Kikuko. My father, sister and brother passed from this world without receiving government acknowledgement or any apology for the quality of life each was forced to endure.

I attribute the early deaths of my siblings and my father to the stressful life they each experienced. From my standpoint, the meagre $21,000 individual payments, even with the government's public acknowledgement of the unjust treatment of some twenty-two thousand individuals, did not begin to compensate for the damage done to families.

I was thankful at least that my sister Keiko, married to Art Miki, then president of the National Association of Japanese Canadians, worked with her husband, members of the redress campaign and our national communities toward finding resolution.

With the loss of each family member, Mother's frustrations and anger, which I believe she had kept hidden from us for years, manifested almost daily through emotionally charged and changing moods. I think it was during these years that she decided to write her memoir, to share with her remaining children and perhaps to help her move on. Mother ended her memoir with the following:

> Is this fate? I have come to feel that it is through generosity and the love of our daughters, sons and friends that we live, and every night I chant the sutra ... and remember the haiku of the famous Ryōkan-san, Chiru Sakura:

ちる	桜		falling sakura,
残る	桜	も	those remaining are also
ちる	桜		falling sakura

> As long as one has breath, there is always death. Obeying the law of the universe, one day the remaining *sakura* [cherry blossoms] will also fall to the ground. Until then, I will spend my last days not worrying too much ... until tomorrow, perhaps.
>
> I will end here.
>
> I would like, before I die, to see the ships in the harbour at Squamish. When I said this, my grandson Mitchell [Toyoaki's son] said there are no longer any ships there—disappointing!

My brother Kenji, the younger of Mother's two sons, passed away from lung cancer during her confinement at Mount Saint Joseph Hospital. Soon after, Mother told me she was no longer taking her high-blood-pressure medication. I did not argue. As a mother, I understood. She had had enough. A strong-willed person, she had expressed to me her hope to die in her sleep, and so she did. She left this world on December 24, 2002, at the age of eighty-nine.

By the end of her life, Mother had resolved the frustrations she had carried for many years, supported by her Buddhist faith, as she chanted the sutra daily before the *butsudan* (family portable shrine), acknowledging the ephemerality of life while at the same time putting behind her the many sad memories that had haunted her life. Only Keiko and I remain of her five children.

On the brighter side, there are the grandchildren that Mother and Father were very proud of. I know she would want me to share her stories with them and their family members.

They are: her first daughter Kikuko's two sons and one daughter, Timothy, Leslie and Brenda; her second daughter Eiko's two sons, Michael and David; her first son Toyoaki's one son, Mitchell; her second son Kenji's one son, Mark; and her third daughter Keiko's two sons and one daughter, Geoffrey, Tani and Jonathan.

Living in Vancouver, Mother was close to her grandsons Mitchell and Mark, Toyoaki's and Kenji's sons, respectively. My sister Keiko and I, living in Winnipeg through those years, raising our respective families, lost touch with them. We are still trying to locate them.

PART THREE

MOTHER'S DAY

Daughter reminiscences (Mother's Day, 2003):

Today is Mother's Day. Notwithstanding that I am not into commercially driven holidays and have never celebrated them as such, even as certainly I am a proud mother of two incredible sons and grandma to five beautiful grandchildren, today I find myself acknowledging the day and feeling a bit lonely.

My younger son, living in Japan, telephoned me to wish me a happy Mother's Day, and my son in Winnipeg sent me a beautiful bouquet of flowers. I am blessed indeed. But since many of my friends are joining their families for dinner and neither of my sons or grandchildren live near me, and this Mother's Day is the first I am without my own mother, it is turning into a day of contemplation.

Mother's passing on December 24, 2002, was an unexpected shock. She had regained energy and was beginning to take an interest again in friends and community affairs. Since I was not worrying about her, I had decided to spend the holiday season, as usual, visiting my son Michael and his family, and my sister Keiko and her family, in Winnipeg. Mother was planning to spend Christmas in Vancouver with her granddaughter Brenda and her grandson Leslie.

When my daughter-in-law Donna phoned to say there was a call for me from the German-Canadian Care Home informing of Mother's death, my son and I and two of my grandchildren were doing some last-minute Christmas shopping. Since nothing could be accomplished by rushing back to Vancouver on Christmas Day, my sister Keiko and I decided we would leave on Boxing Day to begin attending to Mother's funeral arrangements.

We had our family Christmas dinner at my son's home, as usual joined by my sister Keiko and her husband, Art, and their family members. The major celebration of Christmas this year was that it was the first for my grandson Isaac, who was born April 29. At eight months old, dressed in a Santa outfit, he looked a bit bewildered as he was passed from one set of arms to another, held most possessively by his older siblings, Sarah and Samuel.

We participated in our annual Christmas morning ritual, with the family members sitting by the tree in the living room, handing out and opening gifts, and then having breakfast together, prepared by Michael. Our Christmas is usually a very merry affair enjoyed with the children, and this year was no different. My younger son, David, who lives in Japan, was not present,

Sawae, 1994. On December 24, 2002, Sawae passed away at the age of eighty-nine. She was buried with her husband's ashes in accordance with their wishes. Author's personal collection

but there were gifts from him and his wife, Mary Ann, and their son, Jamil, my grandson, and merry Christmas phone calls were exchanged.

This morning, as I sat contemplating the past few years, I remembered that my niece Brenda had telephoned the evening before asking if I would like to go for a walk and out for dinner. She was thinking on Mother's Day of her own mother, my older sister, Kikuko, as well as her grandma, and might also have been feeling a bit of loneliness. So we decided to go to their gravesites with flowers. It was a beautiful day and the cemetery was filled with people, with cars driving in and out. It is interesting what a gravesite can mean to us. It is a symbolic site, a place where one can go to visit a loved one spiritually.

Father's ashes, stored in the Vancouver Buddhist temple mausoleum, were removed and buried with Mother's upon her death. This was in accordance with their wishes, the burial site already purchased and arranged by them.

Mother always had a *butsudan*, a portable shrine most Buddhist families own where offerings are placed each day to ancestors. By the time she died, Mother, sadly, had placed not only photos of her and her husband's parents, but also photos of her husband, her daughter Kikuko and her two sons, Toyoaki and Kenji, in front of the *butsudan*, where she offered prayers daily, chanting the sutra, which she knew by heart.

Keiko and I had held a special family service at the temple to mark Mother's forty-ninth day of passing, the end of her journey to nirvana, but I have done nothing more to date.

So after visiting the gravesites, Brenda and I went to Mandeville's in Burnaby and had lunch there, enjoying leisurely time looking at things pertaining to gardening, then drove to Granville Island, where we did more walking. It was a perfect afternoon with my dear niece.

Tonight, I find myself reminiscing and acknowledging to myself the inadequacy of the mothering I have offered my two sons. But for the first time I recognize that the quality of mothering, including the one that I received from my own mother through her years of struggle, is related to the conditions and situations in which each of us is born, is raised and has lived. Mothering is not only about love. But love is what keeps us alive and together.

Today, I remember Mother as a strong force in my life. She was a strong-willed woman with a lot of power over each of us, including Father, who had been raised as the youngest son in his family. I think her strength came from her secure childhood in Japan as a middle child, one of three sisters, always in competition with her older sister, both of them excelling in schoolwork and given a lot of reinforcement by their parents. Her father, older, was into his second marriage, with a history of having visited, worked and prospered in Canada.

While her marriage to Father was arranged, I think it was a relatively happy one, especially in the early years. The disruption to their lives in 1942 shattered their hopes and dreams. My memories of my parents, particularly in their later years, are largely of Mother's frustrations and bitterness and Father's quiet acceptance.

Undoubtedly, though, Mother had lived with many moments of enjoyment, since she was creative and always strove toward accomplishments, excelling at whatever she did. Upon her death, left among her things were notes and recollections, some haiku and *shigin* poetry, bits of practised calligraphy and at least a dozen years of diaries. She had likely thrown the earlier ones away because of their weight, as the family moved from one place to another, while still retaining many memories, as revealed in the minute details offered in her memoir.

My first son, Michael, was not yet three years old in 1963 when Father and Mother left Winnipeg to live the rest of their lives in Vancouver. It must have been a difficult decision for them to make, since I know they were enjoying time spent with their first two grandchildren, Kikuko's first son, Timothy, and Michael, born a few months later.

I have to admit, I felt a great burden of responsibility lifted from my shoulders when Mother left Winnipeg even as I missed her presence. We wrote to each other and spoke on the phone whenever there was something she wanted to talk over with me. Often, I felt she forgot her worries once she had shared them with me, while I continued to fret about them.

Even though my Japanese immigrant mother did her best to keep up with the times when I was young, sewing clothing for me based on styles she saw in catalogues and magazines, I felt like a country bumpkin compared with the other girls at school. They wore currently stylish clothes, with accessories they knew how to choose for themselves: sweaters with a little scarf, jewellery around their necks and bracelets on their wrists.

Feeling like a misfit, I became a Pollyanna (without knowing this term at the time). I was always anxious to please, so I was well liked wherever I went. I showed a lot of compassion for people around me and tried to be generous and kind. In fact, Mother said I was too friendly, and she worried that would get me into trouble. But such qualities were engendered by the discrimination I was enduring.

I didn't change this attitude until I was well into my marriage. One day, however, I decided that making a constant effort to please others, pretending everything was right in the world, was like apologizing to others, something I realized finally I had no need to do. It took me a while to understand that racist people, those who need to discriminate, were the ones with the problem, not me. They were the ones lacking in self-esteem, needing someone to look down upon in order to raise themselves.

After many years and experiences, I had begun to find pride and comfort in my own skin. I was who I was, and I would try to live my life into the future accordingly.

ART AS A WAY OF LIFE

To analyze my own situation, and in order to move forward, I needed tools, so I began taking basic arts courses, such as sociology, psychology, history, literature and political studies, at University of Winnipeg evening classes.

I had continued to work throughout my marriage, mainly out of choice but also since during the first few years of our marriage, my husband had made the decision to move from studies in engineering to becoming an educator. During this period, after my first son was born, I had become a legal secretary, which was more challenging but which I came to enjoy. (I remember taking my first son, when he was only three or four years old, to the law office during my holiday period to proudly introduce him to my boss and my new office friends.)

My introduction to visual art came around this time. In the late 1960s I was asked by a friend to join her in an art class held in the basement of the church where her brother was the minister. Without much thought, I went with her. She quit soon after, but I stayed on, discovering a new self, a new way of self-expression. I decided to apply to the University of Manitoba School of Art, submitting, as required, a portfolio of work that I quickly put together. By some miracle I was accepted, and my art career began. I registered for the term beginning in 1973.

I was soon to discover that making art was not so easy. It took time for me to realize that art is not just about creating but also about finding one's place; the journey is not limited to one's own history but is about expanding one's thoughts through sharing with others. Art is solely about living—living and doing without necessarily having to consciously interpret, define or choose.

After graduating in 1977 with an honours bachelor of fine arts, majoring in sculpture and drawing, I took another year of study in

Inspired by a desire to connect with her cultural roots, Grace studied sculpture and drawing, later focusing her graduate studies in Asian and social histories of art. Author's personal collection

Western art history while sharing a studio with a couple of friends who were also making art.

But the question was always there in the background: Who was I, a Canadian seen by others as an Asian, who as yet had never visited Japan, my ancestral home?

During the second year of my marriage, when my husband and I were expecting our first child, my mother-in-law passed away. She was someone I respected, and I still wish she had been able to spend more time with us and had met and spent time with her two grandsons. After her passing, my husband and I moved in with my father-in-law in his home in River Heights, where we celebrated the birth of our first son, Michael. My father-in-law was born in Scotland, on the Isle of Lewis, and was working for a major grain industry company at that time. After his retirement, he visited Scotland, then went back again and married a friend from his younger days who was also widowed. Soon after, my husband and I and our two sons visited my father-in-law and his wife in their Glasgow home, along with relatives in Girvan in Ayrshire and in Edinburgh. My father-in-law and his wife visited us in Winnipeg as well, at our home in Fort Garry.

But Japan was not yet in my sight.

Feeling the need to investigate my cultural roots, I continued my education, this time registering at the University of British Columbia (UBC) in 1980 for a two-year graduate studies program in Asian art history.

Surprisingly, I found myself taking more interest in Chinese art history than in Japanese art history. Perhaps I saw the roots of Japanese art in Chinese art (which dates back thousands of years before any documentation of Japanese or Western art).

During my studies at UBC, I travelled back and forth whenever possible to keep up with my family in Winnipeg. But I remember very clearly my son Michael, who had just started his own university education, incredibly once driving all the way from Winnipeg to Vancouver to visit me. As we sat at a restaurant talking and eating a bucket of clams, I realized how grown up he already was, though he was, relatively speaking, still a child. I believe he saw in me someone who was changing, and I felt supported by him.

My studies in Asian art history were having a positive effect on me. My focus had always been to become "Canadian," that is, accepted by others, which seemed impossible at times. I now found myself, through this study, becoming proud of my ancestry.

Even so, since Japanese culture and my ancestry had offered me little comfort to date, it was not surprising that while living in Vancouver as a student, I did not seek out Japanese Canadian friends. I felt more comfortable interacting with those doing graduate studies in Western art. As graduate students, we had many opportunities to meet and interact, as we were hired as student aids. The friends I made during this period, both in class and in residence, remain with me, some still in contact, others in fond memory.

Upon returning to Winnipeg from UBC in the fall of 1982, I informed my husband and then our two sons about the difficult decision I had made to leave my marriage and our family life together, to continue my journey toward self-realization. I wonder today how I could have done this, particularly considering how deeply it affected my sons; the older was in university by then, but the younger was still in high school and was very upset with my decision. However, I left my sons living with their father, without their mother's constant presence, while I—in retrospect, I think, selfishly—concentrated on developing myself. I still have the letters I received from my sons while I was studying at UBC, and rereading them always fills me with tears.

No doubt I felt unqualified to be a good mother to my two sons, who were growing stronger each day, surpassing their mother in identity and focus.

In trying to analyze why I eventually chose art as a path toward resolution, I now realize that it had always been present in my life, except that it had not been called art, per se, but was merely accepted as a way of life.

In my memories of the internment years, I recall Mother going for walks in the woods and coming home with an armful of what I believe was birch bark, which she peeled into thin sheets. She would flatten and dry these sheets and proceed to write on them, with a pointed brush, Japanese poetry and Japanese adages, which she often cited in scolding us children. I also remember her saying she was writing on these sheets to her younger sister, Hideyo, in Japan, someone she obviously missed. Of course, the sheets would have been impossible to mail in those days.

Mother's art, or her way of life, was certainly based in her cultural roots, but it also expressed itself through her interest in sewing.

Sewing was something all Japanese Canadian mothers did in those days as a necessity, to ensure children were dressed properly and to make over old clothes into new ones. The suits Father wore to work in Vancouver were later turned into dress clothes for my brothers. Nothing was wasted—*mottai nai* (too precious to throw away).

But for Mother, it was not just sewing but also designing that she enjoyed. She had been privileged as a young woman, allowed to leave

Opposite: Grace in one of several gowns designed and made by her mother, for whom sewing was not only a necessary skill but a form of artistic expression. Author's personal collection

her home village to attend a women's school in Wakayama City where she studied the domestic arts. After she married Father, she continued with her sewing lessons in Vancouver and even in Minto, where she discovered Mrs. Watada, who had graduated from one of Vancouver's prestigious sewing schools. Mother took design lessons from her. I still recall watching Mother throw a heavy roll of brown paper on the floor with a flourish and then begin drawing the pattern for her next project. Her sewing machine and the beautiful dark wooden measuring square she used to draw patterns with were two things we were not allowed to touch as children.

When I look at early family photographs, I find it remarkable that we are all wearing Western clothes my mother made for us, evidence of her quick adaptation to Canada in the less than five years since her arrival.

As a teenager and then a young woman in Winnipeg, whether attending the annual Christmas ball sponsored by the Manitoba Japanese Canadian Citizens' Association or a university prom, I was always dressed beautifully in gowns Mother had designed and sewn for me. What I learned from this was that one could draw a picture, select the right material and produce a piece of art.

❧

After I returned home to Winnipeg in 1982, I was offered a job as assistant director/curator at the University of Manitoba School of Art's Gallery 1.1.1. (whose archive included the Lionel LeMoine FitzGerald Study Collection). Renting an apartment nearby, I stayed for seven years at this job, working alongside Winnipeg artists and interacting with nationally recognized directors and curators of the time. I also taught one art history class per term and had the opportunity to join students and instructors on their annual field trips to major art galleries in New York, Chicago and Minneapolis. Holidays were spent largely on trips to Europe (London, Amsterdam, Munich, Paris, Milan, Venice, Florence, etc.), visiting museums and galleries. These were years filled with new acculturation experiences.

The artworks hanging in my apartment today remind me of the

many friendships I developed with noted Winnipeg artists, and my shelves contain catalogues of exhibitions I joyfully curated.

During this time, I completed an arts management course at the Banff Centre, which I found useful. It was an interesting experience, as I met not only students from across the country but also international ones, many already holding professional positions in the art world. I also freelance curated an exhibition of works by a talented Toronto artist, Natalka Husar, entitled *Milk and Blood* (1988), at the Floating Curatorial Gallery at Women in Focus, in Vancouver. It was a revelation to look and listen, and to learn, about the struggles experienced by Ukrainian immigrants.

(Interestingly, I did not curate a single exhibition of works by a Japanese Canadian artist during these years. In fact, the only Japanese Canadian artist I knew of at that time was Takao Tanabe, who was fast rising to become one of Canada's major landscape painters. Through my friendship with his sister, Sakaye Tanabe, in Winnipeg, I had previously been introduced to the watercolour paintings, or *sumi-e*, her brother had produced during his visit to Japan, some of which were framed and hanging on her walls. I recall being amazed when Tak, as he was called then, returned from studies in Europe sporting a goatee and wearing a beret! The extent of my own interest in art was not yet apparent.)

It was during this period that I was offered an eye-opening experience that forced me to look beyond the personal issues I had been obsessed with. Soon after Gallery 1.1.1. hired me, I was invited to act as an art adviser to the Inuit printmakers at the Sanavik Co-operative in Baker Lake, then in the Northwest Territories (now in Nunavut). A new friend, the photographer William Eakin, recommended me for the position he was leaving, and he took me to Baker Lake and introduced me to the co-operative's manager, Thomas Iksiraq. Taking this position meant that I would fly to Baker Lake, about 1,600 kilometres due north of Winnipeg, two or three times a year for a few days to advise the co-operative on the choice of drawings for its annual print collection to be offered to the Canadian Eskimo Arts Council.

Meeting the Inuit artists and their families was an emotional experience for me. Looking into their faces, I felt related to them. I spent

many happy hours at the co-operative learning about distinguished artists such as Luke Anguhadluq, Jessie Oonark, William Noah and Marion
Tuu'luq and meeting Simon Tookoome, Ruth Annaqtuusi Tulurialik,
Janet and Hannah Kigusiuq, Victoria Mamnguqsualuk and others, becoming acquainted with their incredible artwork of drawings, prints
and wall hangings. And I spent many hours with Thomas Iksiraq, the
respected manager.

I had the privilege, too, of being introduced to this region and
exploring its empty (though full) landscapes, covered with snow or with
moss depending on the season. There were no trees, but I was surprised
to find blueberries on low-lying bushes, frozen in the snow. I remember
being invited one bright, early spring evening to join friends who were
gathering to close down the shelters over the fishing holes they had
created on frozen Baker Lake, getting ready for the change in season.
These are only a few of the many incredible experiences I was privileged
to take part in.

However, in working and meeting with the Canadian government's Eskimo Arts Council, I realized that while a major industry of
Inuit art was flourishing in the South, with drawings, prints and stone
sculptures bought and sold by collectors and exhibited in galleries and
museums, and with Inuit art history being taught among university
courses, the displaced Inuit communities of artists and their families I
met and saw in Baker Lake were living with their future still at risk, their
art controlled by decisions made by the council.

The Eskimo Arts Council jury members made the final decisions
as to which stonecut prints (as well as which woodcuts, a method that
had been introduced by southern artists, in particular a Japanese immigrant printmaking artist/instructor, Noboru Sawai) were worthy of
receiving the council's seal to become part of the annual collection of
prints sold in the South. The prints that did not meet with the council's
approval were ordered to be destroyed. I was shocked when I discovered
this, and before I left my advisory position, I spoke against this meth-
odology as colonial, unfair to the artists and the printmakers, and suggested that the prints rejected by the council jury be sold in the North
to benefit the North.

༄

After seven years at Gallery 1.1.1., I applied for and was granted a leave. I felt the need to upgrade my knowledge of art theories and practices that were undergoing major changes (postmodernism, post-colonialism, etc.), which I had not had the time to seriously investigate.

The year was 1990, and with my Japanese Canadian Redress compensation in hand to cover the costs of tuition and residency (in memory of my parents, who were not financially able to offer me such an education), I enrolled in a graduate studies program under the renowned feminist scholar Dr. Griselda Pollock at the University of Leeds in northern England. I had met Dr. Pollock a year earlier when I attended a workshop she led at the Vancouver Art Gallery. I visited Leeds soon after and decided to pursue studies there.

Before leaving for England, I made a side trip to New York with a friend to take in a major exhibition that was advertised at the time. Then I flew to Japan to visit my son, who was teaching English in Aichi Prefecture. This was my first trip to Japan. My son David and I travelled to Mio, my parents' birthplace in Wakayama Prefecture, where we met Mother's younger sister, my aunt Hideyo.

A few years earlier, my older son, Michael, had also taught at an English-language school in Japan. After graduating from law school, he had taken a year off before proceeding to article, travelling through Europe and the Middle East for half the year, then going on to Japan for the second half. David, following in his brother's footsteps, made arrangements to teach at the same school, and that is where I visited him. A few years after returning home to Canada, David received an invitation from two instructors, one British, the other Japanese, to join them in establishing an English-language school in Toyohashi/Toyokawa in Aichi Prefecture. That is where he settled and still lives today, married, with one son, Jamil Kenji.

In visiting New York, Tokyo and then London at that time, I noticed major cultural differences, revealed perhaps most tellingly by the cities' busy train stations. The New York and London train stations were absolutely filthy, while the Tokyo train station was spotless.

Interestingly, I learned that my grandson in Japan was periodi-
cally required to take an extra shirt and gloves to school. Students were
sent out to streets around the school to pick up debris for an hour or so.
No wonder the city itself was so tidy, with no graffiti or scribbling on the
walls or garbage strewn on the sidewalks—not uncommon sights here
in Canada. Children are taught from grade-school age to respect their
environment.

The only regret I had about leaving Winnipeg for Leeds at that
time was that I was leaving behind my first grandchild, my beautiful
granddaughter Sarah, born only the year before. I was already a proud
grandmother and enjoying time spent with her.

My studies at the University of Leeds were not easy. I had to get
back into a heavy schedule of attending classes and researching and
writing papers, while living in an international student residence with
other graduate and postgraduate students.

As usual, I was the oldest among my peers, both in class and in
residence. In those days, whenever anyone asked how old I was, I would
respond, "Why do you need to know? I don't live according to age." I had
not begun my studies until my two sons were of school age, so age could
not be a concern if I was to fulfill my dreams of self-realization.

Between writing papers, I managed to take a few trips, to a gallery
in Manchester and to London once a month for a day or two. While
studying, I admit, I often watched tennis on TV, wondering why at my
age I was focused on studies in a room in a student residence instead
of enjoying Wimbledon. It had been a long time since I'd played tennis
myself. In my late teens through my early twenties in Winnipeg, I had
been obsessed with playing tennis every weekend with friends, as soon
as the outdoor courts at Sargent Park opened in May.

But this was a special year for me. I was able to interact with
national and international students in class and in residence, and I
learned a lot from them, particularly regarding how their various ethnic
and cultural backgrounds dictated their lives.

During this period the Gulf War broke out, so it was a difficult
time for the Middle Eastern students. It was also a year of major pro-
tests and social movements organizing against Margaret Thatcher

and her government. I remember rushing out of my residence to join demonstrations with camera in hand. Though I was an international student, I was sent an invoice to pay the poll tax, which I ignored. My friends joked that I might never be able to visit England again without being arrested.

After a little more than twelve months of study, I graduated with a master's in the social history of art in 1991. My choice of study in Leeds under Dr. Pollock had not been entirely about academic advancement but was related to the continuing investigation of myself not only as a Canadian of Asian ancestry but also now as a woman who, along with many others, was facing various kinds of discrimination and misogynistic behaviour, particularly in the workplace. Issues I thought I had managed carefully in the past came to light upon my return to Winnipeg.

As I was getting ready to return to Canada, I received a letter from the then director of the University of Manitoba School of Art, informing me that the position of assistant director/curator at Gallery 1.1.1., which I had held for seven years and had been offered a leave from on the condition that I return to the position, was now closed to me for "economic reasons." This news was, of course, unexpected, but with this turn of events, I discovered (or began to acknowledge) that people in power positions—mostly men in those days—did whatever they wanted to benefit themselves without caring about others, particularly women outside of their own personal spheres.

This was a period when men in management or teaching positions, many of them married, were known to have affairs with their young female students or employees, behaviour largely ignored or accepted. I learned from reliable sources that many complaints lodged by women were sitting in administrative and union files. Having taken part in the university, both administratively and as part of the teaching staff, watching and listening from the sidelines, this was not news to me.

While this was not part of the grievance I filed through the employees' union, there was no doubt that during the seven years I had worked at the School of Art, I had myself experienced misogynistic behaviour by the school's management.

In relation to my termination from the gallery, I received words of support from respected members of the university's higher levels of academic management and governance, whom I had met through my work. Even though they were not able to offer actual assistance, since I had already filed a complaint with the union, I was grateful for their words of support. Several members of the artist community also openly opposed the unjust treatment, with one major artist even cancelling an exhibition of her work that had been planned at the gallery. There was local media coverage of the event, and the then director of the Department of Architecture sympathetically offered me part-time work teaching art history to fill the gap while I awaited resolution.

Despite all this support, however, after attending various meetings and listening to (largely male) officials and lawyers from both sides discuss the issue, I came to the conclusion that there was no way a woman like me could win a case like this. So, I decided to move forward and applied for the first job I saw advertised. It was a director/curator position at a place called Little Gallery, in the city of Prince Albert, Saskatchewan. It was not an easy thing to do to move out of Winnipeg, where my two sons were living, but I took the job when it was offered.

One thing I regret to this day is that because of these circumstances, I never looked back to the year I spent at the University of Leeds or the thesis I wrote. Recently, I received a query from an art history professor at the University of Manitoba, asking if I had published it and wondering if he could read it, since the topic, based on my interpretation of Lionel LeMoine FitzGerald's self-portraits, was of interest to him and the McMichael Canadian Art Collection in Ontario.

He had learned about the thesis from a member of a small group of female academics who had invited me to do a presentation at a gathering they had put together soon after I had returned from Leeds.

Sadly, I had to go through my filing cabinet to find the thesis, written some thirty years ago.

❧

One of the first people I met in Prince Albert after moving there in 1992 was Poet Laureate John V. Hicks. He came daily to the gallery, located on the second floor of the town hall building, and after a tea break at four o'clock sharp, he pulled the rope that rang the town bell. I remember with great nostalgia that on my first meeting with him, he offered me the privilege of pulling the rope, as he said kindly, to announce my arrival. In addition to this warm welcome from him, a large, friendly welcome party was put on for me by board members and the exceptionally talented artist and artisan communities, with coverage in the local media. Jack Hicks and I, along with a few local artists (including the painter George Glenn), met regularly from then on, spending many happy and memorable hours together.

One day, during our afternoon tea break in the gallery's kitchen, we noticed that the sky was bright and sunny but rain had begun to fall. I said to Jack, "I believe there is a fox's wedding taking place." Calling a sun shower a "fox's wedding" (*kitsune no yomeiri*) was something Mother had taught me from Japanese folklore about a supernatural event. Jack was very interested, and within a couple of days he had written a poem based on this legend and had sent it to me.

I spent three years at the Little Gallery curating works by local artists and artists from around the province, as well as teaching a course in art history at the University of Saskatchewan. Some of the local artists were interested in the new thinking about postmodern theories that I had studied at the University of Leeds, so we held a few sessions that allowed me to get to know each of them and to appreciate their interests.

During this time, I was again led to question some accepted practices in Canadian society. I was introduced to many noteworthy Saskatchewan artists through the gallery in Prince Albert, but I noticed soon after I had arrived that none of the many Indigenous artists in the province were included in the gallery's activities. In preparing for the following year's Annual Juried Art Festival exhibition, I met with Indigenous artists and encouraged them to submit their work. In the process, I learned of a few artists being held in Prince Albert's penitentiary and went there to visit them (a sad but incredible experience). They were impressive artists creating beautiful works.

This major change in the gallery's policy was supported generally by the existing artist community, if not by all board members at first.

Several artworks by Indigenous artists were included in the following year's festival exhibition, one of them winning the Bank of Montreal award for most popular work.

During my third year at the Little Gallery, I worked with the late Bob Boyer, a well-known visual artist who was also a professor at what was then called the Saskatchewan Indian Federated College at the University of Regina. We produced a successful travelling exhibition, *Separate Identities: Sharing Worlds*, curated by Bob and featuring works by many already established Cree, Saulteaux, Nakoda, Dakota, Chipewyan and Métis artists and writers, supported by the Saskatchewan Arts Board.

I have many emotional memories of the few years I spent in Prince Albert. I left with several pieces of artwork, including a coffee table made by Adrian Vinish and a little paper box made by George Glenn, offered to me as a birthday greeting. There were many artisans and craftspeople in the area, and I have a set of blue ceramic bowls, bought just before I left, that I still use regularly, always with enjoyment.

One of the gallery's volunteers, Karen Cay, an undergraduate student at the time, offered me a copy of a paper she had carefully researched and written. Incredibly, after all the history I had (self-centredly) focused on, this was my first introduction to residential schools, which had existed shamefully in Canada for many years. I still have the paper, and I'm grateful to Karen for sharing this knowledge with me.

I left Prince Albert during a period when the arts community had received assent from the city to build a new space for a combined art gallery and playhouse. I often think I would like to visit this community of artists again.

RETURN TO VANCOUVER

My next move was to Vancouver, where my aging mother was living, in 1994. Ten years had passed since Father's death, and Mother was living alone in the Kinsmen apartment for seniors on Commercial Drive. I decided to look into any jobs that might allow me to be near her.

The Vancouver Art Gallery (VAG) and the Burnaby Art Gallery were each advertising a curatorial position at the time. I was short-listed by the VAG, but the interview was uncomfortable. It consist-ed largely of questions related to art practices and theories, posed by three male curatorial and management staff, which I had no real problem answering. A few days later, I received a phone call asking about the references I had given them, so I knew I was still being considered. However, I posed a couple of questions to them: Were they not interested in what I was personally bringing to their gallery, if they were considering hiring me? Had they not noticed that I was "different" during the interview?

It had become important to me that this "difference," something I had for years tried to erase from my life, be recognized and appreci-ated. Of course, the person who had phoned me regarding references was not in charge of the situation. However, I heard nothing further from the VAG.

During my visit to Vancouver for the VAG interview, I informed the Burnaby Art Gallery that I was in town. Soon after my interview with this gallery, I was informed that I was hired. And so started a new era of taking up residence in Vancouver, the city where I had begun my life many years ago.

My last visit to Vancouver had been a couple of years before, in 1992, when I attended the National Association of Japanese Canadians (NAJC) Homecoming Conference, which celebrated the Japanese Canadian

Redress of September 22, 1988. It was held at the Hotel Vancouver, a venue once closed to residents of Asian ancestry.

At the conference, I learned that in early 1977, the year of the Japanese Canadian Centennial celebration, Vancouver City Council had approved in principle a Land Use Plan and a Concept Plan allocating funds in the amount of $685,000 to the Downtown Eastside area, of which the Japanese Canadian community was to receive $150,000 as encouragement to preserve and expand their culture and facilities. Under the city's Policy 13, Historical Importance of Area, a clause was inserted that "the historical importance of the area be recognized."

On April 16, with the support of the City of Vancouver, some seventy Issei seniors came together to plant twenty-one *sakura* trees in Oppenheimer Park (which we called "Powell Ground" in the old days) to celebrate the 100th anniversary of Canada's first known immigrant from Japan. I was happy that my parents were able to attend (likely through their membership in Tonari Gumi, founded in 1974 as a centre for Japanese Canadians to gather and for elders and newcomers to receive services and advice). The *sakura* trees remain, beside the cedar trees, as living reminders for future generations.

The 1992 Homecoming Conference was my first introduction to the national communities of Japanese Canadians who had gathered for this celebration. Of particular interest for me at this event were the artists. Coming from various points across the nation, they expressed the common view that there was a need for a gathering to allow artists to identify and connect with one another. Before 1942, most of these artists' families had lived on the West Coast. The internment and then the dispersal order had scattered them across the country.

Led by Bryce Kanbara, a noted artist/curator from Hamilton, Ontario, the artists attending the conference made a proposal to the NAJC to hold a national gathering on the arts. Funding was granted.

In April 1994, Toronto artists held their eastern regional conference, titled Ai (Love): A Symposium for Japanese Canadians in the Arts. A print directory of Japanese Canadian professional artists was compiled in 1994 by the artist Aiko Suzuki. (More recently, the online Japanese Canadian Artists Directory, built on the 1994 print directory, was

The First Powell Street Festival during the 1977 Japanese Canadian Centennial. The Festival celebrates the history of Japanese Canadians. In addition to being a platform for Japanese Canadian arts performers to showcase their talents, the festival engages the broader community through fun cultural activities, volunteer opportunities, and of course, delicious food. City of Vancouver Archives; Paul Yee fonds. 2008-010.0187

created collaboratively by the Powell Street Festival Society in Vancouver, the Japanese Canadian Cultural Centre in Toronto and the NAJC.)

Vancouver artists held their western regional conference, titled *Tsudoi*/Gatherings: Japanese Canadians in the Arts, a year later in March 1995, dedicating it to the memory of the BC artist and poet Roy Kiyooka.

I had only recently accepted and moved to the curatorial position at the Burnaby Art Gallery, and at that time I knew few Japanese Canadians, let alone artists, living in Vancouver. Incredibly, however, I was invited to organize the western regional conference. I was likely recommended by Bryce Kanbara and the Vancouver artist Haruko Okano, both of whom I had met at the Homecoming Conference. It was a great honour and privilege, especially since through this work I was introduced to the many Japanese Canadian artists working in western Canada, particularly in British Columbia.

(Worth mentioning here is the Japanese Canadian Art and Artists Symposium held some twenty years later on April 2, 2016, at the Japanese Canadian Cultural Centre in Toronto. Bryce Kanbara, now the curator and proprietor of You Me Gallery in Hamilton, in his role as curator and chair of the Japanese Canadian Cultural Centre Arts Committee, invited me and Haruko Okano to be keynote speakers at the symposium. With such leadership as offered by Bryce, it is evident that some two decades after the Homecoming Conference, Japanese Canadian artists have taken their rightful place in Canadian and international art circles. The urgency to connect with one another felt in 1992 is no longer an issue.)

Another invitation I received shortly after I moved to Vancouver was from the now late Jim Wong-Chu, who invited me to work with him and his group to produce Asian Heritage Month. Founded in 1996, the initiative continues in Vancouver to this day. Jim put great effort into producing this yearly event. It was entirely a new experience for me (coming from the Prairies), to work cross-culturally, especially within a large Asian Canadian community.

As curator of the Burnaby Art Gallery, my focus quickly moved to developing and exhibiting works with cross-cultural themes, supported by the then director of the gallery, Karen A. Henry. A series of exhibitions in 1997 under the title *Cultural Migrations and Difference*, subtitled *Tracing Cultures I, II, III and IV*, featured eight artists, among whom were immigrants from both Europe and Asia as well as artists born and raised in Canada, including Indigenous artists. We also produced an exhibition of artworks and a catalogue of texts by local public school students (led by the then gallery educator, Rita Wong), many of them children of recent immigrants.

One of the participating artists in the *Tracing Cultures* series was Haruko Okano, a Canadian of Japanese ancestry who, having been raised by non-Japanese foster parents, was dealing with issues of authenticity through meditational art and practices. Another participant was Gu Xiong, who had emigrated from China soon after the Tiananmen Square Massacre in 1989. Also included were an Ojibwe artist (Dolleen Manning), a visiting Chinese artist (He Gong) and Canadians of eastern

European (Branko Djuras and Taras Polataiko), Persian (Zainub Verjee) and Chinese (JJ Lee) heritage.

I curated several solo exhibitions at the gallery during this period, including an installation by Henry Tsang, recipient of the 1993 VIVA Award from the Jack and Doris Shadbolt Foundation. Another installation, this one focusing on ceramics by Sadashi Inuzuka, a Japanese immigrant artist, was based on an environmental theme and titled *Dear Lake* (referencing Deer Lake, located next to the Burnaby Art Gallery).

Tied to the United Nations' Fourth World Conference on Women in 1995, we mounted an exhibition titled *Through Women's Eyes*, which was accompanied by discussions of current social issues led by those who had attended the conference in Beijing.

My art education, begun in the '70s essentially to find myself, had by the '90s led me through more than fifteen years of curatorial practice in contemporary art, focusing on cross-cultural artists and themes. These were years of truly remarkable learning for me. Through meeting and working with various communities of artists, focusing often by chance on post-colonial issues of selective exclusion, I was offered not only new knowledge but also opportunities to build enough confidence to invite, and to share, my own experiences with others.

When the Burnaby Art Gallery changed from a non-profit public institution to a city gallery in 1998, though I was invited to remain and was offered the position of director/curator, I left within a year. I found it difficult to work under male bureaucratic control. Unfortunately this was not to be my last experience dealing with such issues.

SHIFT TO
MUSEUM PRACTICE

While I was working as curator at the Burnaby Art Gallery, I heard that a Japanese Canadian National Museum was in the developmental stage and that volunteers and part-time workers were collecting archival materials, including interviews and photographs, at the Greater Vancouver Japanese Canadian Citizens' Association building at 511 East Broadway in Vancouver.

When I also heard of plans for the construction of a Nikkei Heritage Centre in Burnaby, which was to include rental space for the Japanese Canadian National Museum, I immediately visited the office where the plans were being made, even as I wondered why this centre was being built in the city of Burnaby—as Mother had remarked, Burnaby was not the centre of Japanese Canadian activities before 1942; Vancouver was.

My thoughts then were that I might be able to offer some consultation assistance through my long years of experience with institutional practices and my interest in our Japanese Canadian history. However, after a visit with the administrative staff, I never heard back. At the time, I still knew only a few Japanese Canadians living on the West Coast, so perhaps I was treated as a stranger, my background ignored.

However, a few years later in 1998, I was approached by the then president of the board of the museum in the making, Frank Kamiya, for professional consultation in producing a museum that meets national standards, to open at the proposed site in Burnaby on September 22, 2000. With this request (which came at an opportune time, since I had just left the Burnaby Art Gallery and was contemplating freelance curatorial work), my life took a major turn from art to focus on Japanese Canadian history and museum practice.

I offered volunteer time for close to a year in researching all that was needed to establish a national-standard museum, consulting in particular with (the now late) Dr. Michael Ames, emeritus professor of anthropology at the University of British Columbia, who had invited me to take part on a panel when I first met him at a BC Museums Association conference. I also consulted with curatorial and management staff at the Vancouver Museum and the Vancouver Holocaust Education Centre, receiving much information and advice.

To begin the process of applying for grants to produce the various museum programs, it became clear the organization needed to fill the official position of director/curator. So, in June 1999, I was appointed executive director/curator and was offered two days' pay per week of $300, which was all the museum board could afford at that time.

Of course, this was a full-time job. And the salary offered was certainly not enough for a single person to survive on. Nevertheless, I agreed. I decided to take the opportunity to offer the community my knowledge and expertise to realize this important history preservation and educational project, that is, to develop a Japanese Canadian museum and archive to national standards (particularly since, owing to family circumstances, I had not taken part in the Japanese Canadian Redress campaign in the 1980s).

I immediately began applying for grants from diverse sources to ensure the development of not only a museum, including the exhibition space and a collection storage area with appropriate temperature controls, but also a place where visiting students and scholars could access the archive, that is, a collaborative research centre, with staff assistance.

Very soon, the Japanese Canadian National Museum received official approval, having met the national museum standard requirements.

Our next step was to raise funds to produce an exhibition to be installed in time for the opening date. Not having the funds to hire a professional museum exhibition curator, I took on the job, assisted by part-time staff and volunteers. With community consultations (particularly from Dr. Roy Miki and Dr. Midge Ayukawa), grant applications were made to various sources to cover the exhibition production costs, including design and installation fees and the cost of publishing a catalogue to document the inaugural exhibition.

In the process, I accessed historical photographs and information from private collections and from the Vancouver Public Library's collection, in particular the Leonard Frank/British Columbia Security Commission photographs, as well as from the University of British Columbia's Institute of Asian Research, assisted by Mr. Tsuneharu Gonnami.

As word went out that a Japanese Canadian museum was in development, I was invited to speak at the conferences of both the BC Museums Association and the Canadian Museums Association, addressing in particular the question of why a separate Japanese Canadian museum was felt to be necessary when there were already several national museums in existence. In retrospect, it was a good question and not easily answered, especially for people who had little knowledge of Japanese Canadian history. However, I answered willingly, since I was at that time totally committed to producing a museum—a *Japanese Canadian* museum—based on the history of human justice, to be shared with all Canadians.

The objectives of the museum included membership and audience participation beyond that of its own community. Telling the experiences of Japanese Canadians, particularly the internment and the fight for justice leading to the Japanese Canadian Redress and acknowledgement by the Government of Canada, was central to our first exhibition. These stories told in multi-layers of voices constituted examination of fundamental principles of human rights as practised in Canada.

For instance, the following is an excerpt from *Democracy Betrayed: The Case for Redress*, a submission presented by the National Association of Japanese Canadians to the Government of Canada on the violation of rights and freedoms of Japanese Canadians during and after the Second World War (1984): "The principles of democracy were betrayed when the government, instead of invoking the full force of the law to protect Japanese Canadians against racist agitation, incarcerated the victims of race prejudice and without consent, liquidated properties and belongings to compel the victims to pay for their own internment."

Questions raised in the museum's inaugural exhibition touched on the concepts of citizenship, human rights and multiculturalism and the basic democratic principles upon which we believe our country is based.

Dr. Audrey Kobayashi, in her paper "Racism and Law in Canada: A Geographical Perspective," points out a gap that can exist between principles and practice, as when "the Nuremburg Trials were shocking the world into outrage, when the United Nations was remapping the landscape of human rights, and Canadian representatives were in the forefront of this international moral reconstruction, Canadian citizens could be deported from their own country and treatment legalized in the courts."[6]

The stories pertaining to the internment of Japanese Canadians and the redress settlement experienced by Japanese Canadians are first and foremost Canadian stories. There is an urgency to them being told through the voices of those who experienced the events, because they continue to be pivotal in the consciousness of this community. They relate to a history that speaks to notions of racialization. Japanese Canadians were designated not only as "enemy aliens" but as the "Jap." They were, even before the war began, already registered and were required to carry a registration card, which showed not only their status, whether born in Canada, a naturalized citizen or a national, but also their fingerprints.

Even though Japanese Canadians share a history with other Canadians in geographic space and in time, with our earliest pioneer immigrant recorded as arrived in 1877, at the time when we were opening the Japanese Canadian National Museum, our lives were not reflected in Canadian mainstream museums or in national or provincial school curricula.

The repercussion for all Canadians is that these stories call into question our assumption that we are a country with an impeccable human rights record.

---

6   Audrey Kobayashi, "Racism and Law in Canada: A Geographical Perspective," *Urban Geography* 11, no. 5 (1990): 447–73.

Hundreds attended the ribbon cutting ceremony in celebration of the opening of the Nikkei National Heritage Centre, on September 22, 2000. Author's personal collection

Whether in reference to fishing, farming or mining industries, or as neighbours, or in relation to the politics of our own governments, today or in the past, we were there, participating and contributing. Any differences should only have been heritage differences to be shared and appreciated with all Canadians. But from the beginning, Japanese immigrants encountered racial prejudice directed at all "Orientals."

The Japanese Canadian National Museum and its inaugural exhibition, *Reshaping Memory, Owning History: Through the Lens of Japanese Canadian Redress*, was launched by Frank Kamiya, the museum's founding board president, and myself, its founding executive director/curator, on September 22, 2000, the same day as the opening of the National Nikkei Heritage Centre, with the museum located on the main floor as its tenant.

It was a great event attended by hundreds, with many distinguished guests. I had invited Dr. Michael Ames to offer the keynote address, and he graciously accepted. (He was later to invite me, representing the Japanese Canadian National Museum, to participate in a

Sawae, Grace's son Michael, and Grace's first granddaughter, Sarah, attend the banquet celebrating the opening of the Japanese Canadian National Museum, along with Grace and Michael's wife, Donna. Author's personal collection

panel discussion, "How to Design for and with Many Voices? Two Case Studies," in October 2000. It was part of a conference titled Designing the Future Together, held by the Western and BC Museums Associations in Victoria, BC.)

Important to me personally was that my older son, Michael, together with his wife, Donna, and my first grandchild, Sarah, came from Winnipeg to attend both the opening ceremony and the evening banquet. My mother and my younger brother, Kenji, together with my niece Brenda (the daughter of my older sister, Kikuko), were also able to join us.

My sister Keiko Miki (the forty-day-old baby Mother had carried on the back of a truck to the internment site in 1942), as the then president of the National Association of Japanese Canadians, with her husband, Art Miki, led with others the inaugural ribbon-cutting ceremony of the National Nikkei Heritage Centre.

So it was, for us, not only about the opening of the Japanese Canadian National Museum, but also a memorable family affair.

Reshaping Memories, Owning History: Through the Lens of Japanese Canadian Redress was the inaugural exhibition of the Japanese Canadian National Museum. Author's personal collection

⤳

However, the development of our Japanese Canadian National Museum did not evolve as I, together with the museum's limited and underpaid staff and community volunteers, had optimistically expected. Within the next year we researched and produced, with a community committee, a five-year plan for the continued development of the Japanese Canadian National Museum. This plan was never to surface.

There had been warnings months before the inauguration. While I was working first as a volunteer beginning in 1998 and then as the museum's executive director/curator from 1999, the vice-president of the museum board had begun making critical remarks about my performance at every board meeting. Soon after the museum's inauguration, the vice-president assumed the role of board president and continued to show disrespect for the experience and knowledge of professional staff and volunteers. His remarks clearly revealed his lack of understanding about the role of the board.

When a distinguished professional engineer joined the board, he recognized that the relationship between the board president and the staff was causing damage to the museum's development. He formed a mediating committee with assistance from a few board members and asked for written clarification of the separate roles as understood by the president and by the executive director. The engineer unfortunately left the board for personal reasons, and the board members on the mediating committee resigned at the next annual general meeting.

In spite of my efforts to draw the board's attention to the seriousness of the situation, my relationship with the board president continued to deteriorate. I carried on with developing the museum's programs and applied for operating grants, and, hoping to ease tensions, I developed a workshop to educate the board and staff about their roles. However, it became clear there would be no solution to the problem as long as the president continued to influence the board.

In 2002, I quit my position as executive director/curator. My loyalty to the mandate of the museum had prevented me from quitting earlier, but by this point I had had enough. It occurred to me that the board members were abiding by the Japanese proverb "The nail that sticks out gets hammered down." Some people in our community believe that such conduct emanates from those damaged by the effects of the internment. But how long can we use this excuse? And why should such damage turn us into bullies, or into followers without courage?

I have travelled the same road and found a voice not only to share personal issues but also to offer support as required, understanding the hardships and struggles each of us, as Japanese Canadians, have experienced.

I have also learned through the years, from personal experience, that women who speak out on issues are more often called troublemakers than problem solvers or peacemakers, while men who do the same are treated and recognized as community leaders. I have come to respect and to accept the word *troublemaker*, used against women, as a compliment.

After leaving my position as the museum's executive director/ curator, I received (and very much appreciated) responses from many national community leaders, historians and artists, as well as from National Association of Japanese Canadians and Greater Vancouver Japanese Canadian Citizens' Association board members, who stepped forward publicly and spoke or published letters of concern, not only on my behalf but out of concern for the well-being of our Japanese Canadian National Museum.

In July 2003, after the museum had merged to become part of the Nikkei Heritage Centre, I was invited by the president of the merged board to complete under contract the two exhibitions I had proposed and had left unfinished when I quit. The substantial funds I had already raised through national grant applications to produce the two proposed exhibitions were on the verge of being lost. The museum's credibility was in jeopardy.

I felt that in order to save the museum I had worked so hard to open and develop, I had little choice but to return to complete the two exhibition projects, particularly as the themes of these exhibitions were important not only to me personally but also for the preservation of Japanese Canadian pre-war history.

One of the exhibitions, titled *Levelling the Playing Field: Legacy of Vancouver's Asahi Baseball Team*, was inspired by Pat Adachi's 1992 documentary book, *Asahi: A Legend in Baseball.* Unfortunately, the funds I had budgeted had been drastically reduced, which resulted in cancelling the stories and artifact catalogue that was intended to accompany the exhibition.

Elmer Morishita and (the now late) George Oikawa, who were members of the board at the time and were knowledgeable about baseball, kindly stepped forward to volunteer their assistance with the project. We worked together to launch the Asahi exhibition at the museum in 2004. The exhibition then travelled to the Museum of Vancouver (formerly the Vancouver Museum) and to a few other venues nationally.

Shashin: Japanese Canadian Photography to 1942 was the title of the second exhibition I had been researching and had left unfinished in 2002. It was organized in partnership with the University of Victoria's Art Department, which had, after a talk I gave at a BC Museums Association conference, invited me to take part in a larger history project it had undertaken, supported by an SSHRC (Social Sciences and Humanities Research Council) grant. Besides financial assistance, I was offered a young staff member to assist in this project.

My research for this exhibition was focused firstly on my interest in the history of the photo studio in the village of Cumberland, on Vancouver Island, which existed between 1880 and 1935. Founded as Hayashi Studio by Senji Hayashi, a Japanese immigrant, it was succeeded by a photographer by the name of Kitamura, and then by Tokitaro Matsubuchi. The photo collections are currently held by the Cumberland Museum.

I had been introduced to these photographs when the late Dr. Midge Ayukawa introduced me to a book by the Japanese journalist/author Miyoko Kudo, titled *Maboroshi no Machi, Maboroshi no Onna, Cumberland* (Cumberland: Illusion of a town, illusion of a woman), held in the Asian Studies Library at the University of British Columbia. Kudo used a selection of the Cumberland photographs to support a personal story.

During the research process, my interest soon extended to other photographic studios operating in New Westminster and Vancouver between 1895 and 1942, and also to the independent or freelance photographers who worked along the west coast of British Columbia during this period, documenting various social and occupational activities.

Shashin opened in 2004 at the Royal BC Museum in Victoria. The exhibition then moved to the Japanese Canadian National Museum before travelling to other venues, accompanied by a published catalogue.

Prior to leaving the position of executive director/curator in January 2002, I had given talks on each of the exhibition subjects at conferences, and I had a strong conviction that the themes would be of enough interest to lead to continued research by others. I was right in this. Within a few years, public interest in the Vancouver Asahi story and the historic photo studio of Cumberland had peaked, resulting in related research projects undertaken by noted filmmakers, writers and others.

The Japanese Canadian National Museum, which I had researched and produced with community volunteers and national museum community advice and input, and proudly inaugurated on

September 22, 2000 (the anniversary date of Japanese Canadian Redress), is today known as the Nikkei National Museum, a name that
has little if any meaning for many Japanese Canadians (*nikkei* describes
anyone of Japanese ancestry living abroad).

On a related note, I would like to share the following story. In
2014, when the then consul general of Japan in Vancouver offered a
series of talks related to the history of Japan–Canada relations, I took
the opportunity during question period to ask him how it was that the
Japanese government could declare war on us, knowing that people of
Japanese ancestry were living here in Canada and in the United States.

His response was simple and truthful: "You are not Japanese." I
have not forgotten these words, coming from the mouth of the consul
general of Japan. He is right. We are *not* Japanese. We are *Canadian
citizens*—we should always remember this. Our first loyalty is to this
country, Canada.

I am disappointed that the museum that preserves and archives
our *Japanese Canadian* history, inaugurated as the Japanese Canadian
National Museum, is now called the Nikkei museum. I wonder, how has
its mandate changed?

ᒃᑫ

While I was considering the contract offered to complete the two exhibitions I had been researching when I quit the museum in 2002, I decided to accept an invitation from a friend of Mother's, a Jōdo Shinshū
Buddhist bishop here in Vancouver, to offer a talk at the Nishi Hongwanji's Fifth Gathering for Peace, which was to be held in Shiga Prefecture in December 2003.

I recall with heartfelt thanks the welcome I received from the two
Buddhist priests in Japan. One had spent some time in Alberta several
years before as a student minister; the other, Rev. Tetsuya Uno, had previously visited the Japanese Canadian National Museum to meet with
me. During my visit, Rev. Uno invited me to his own temple in Shiga,
where I met his young family.

I was greeted at the airport, and after staying overnight at the
newly opened Kyoto station hotel, I was picked up the next morning

by Rev. Uno, who took me to the conference site, offering me a tour on the way, in particular, I remember, around the large and beautiful Lake Biwa.

I titled my talk "How Do We Remember the Past? Legacy of the Redress Settlement for Japanese Canadians." I wrote it first in English but decided to deliver it in Japanese, feeling it would be more appropriate, more personal, even though the conference had arranged an interpreter to assist me. I looked to a friend in Vancouver, the respected scholar Tatsuo Kage, to translate the talk for me, and I accompanied the talk with screened photos related to the events I mentioned. I learned (*after* the speech, thank goodness) that while I was speaking into a dark room, there were 840 people in attendance!

It was a great experience for me to present Japanese Canadian history, covering the internment period during the Second World War, through personal, family and community experiences, and the impact of the resolution that followed some years later, the Japanese Canadian Redress campaign and the acknowledgement of injustice offered by the prime minister of Canada on September 22, 1988.

This event and my guest presentation received a lot of publicity in the local media, and I felt honoured to be given such an opportunity to take part in this Gathering for Peace. I enjoyed the wonderful response from the attendees. (Indeed, one man came forward after the talk and told me he was the little boy appearing in one of the screened photos of families being "repatriated" that I had included. He said his mother and siblings had returned to Canada but that he had remained in Japan to this day, married and raising his own family.)

Many people in Japan were not aware of what happened to us here in Canada after Japan attacked Pearl Harbor and Canada declared war on Japan in 1942; they were also unaware of the conditions of racism that existed for Japanese (and other Asian) immigrants prior to 1942. This was my first experience of offering our story to a Japanese public, though in recent years I have been given opportunities to speak whenever I visit Japan, most recently in Osaka and in Tokyo, by academic friends I have met through the years.

The purpose of the Nishi Hongwanji's Gathering for Peace, sponsored by Kyoto's Jōdo Shinshū Buddhist Temple, is to offer penance for the temple's having supported the Imperial Japanese Army during the Pacific War, as explained in the following excerpt from its Declaration: "In August 1994, we conducted the 50th Year Memorial Service for Those Who Perished in World War II regardless of the country of birth, in order to recollect the memory of the dead and to think of survivors' hardship during the war which continued for 15 years. On July 5th 1995, in the following year, we got together in the 1st Gathering for Peace which was held to mark the half-century anniversary of the end of the war and renewed our wish for the world without any wars."

Unforeseen
Consequences

After I left my position as executive director/curator of the Japanese Canadian National Museum in January 2002, I was made aware what stress can lead to. I am close to being a workaholic, but since I had mostly done things I enjoyed, the word *stress* was not part of my vocabulary.

Soon after I quit my job at the museum, I moved to a different apartment in the city and began waking up in the mornings after having bad dreams. I began to think this was part and parcel of the way I had been feeling of late and decided it was to be blamed not on the move, but on the events that had preceded the move that were still haunting the present.

In fall 2002, while I was dealing with the aftermath of my experience at the museum, I began to experience sharp flashes of pain across my right temple and down the side of my nose. Strangely, the pain seemed to be only at the surface, and in the next instant it would pass. Friends suggested that perhaps I had shingles. But the rash that comes with shingles is in the form of blisters. My face was often red in spots with a rash, dry and rough on the surface.

I am normally a very healthy person and, like my father, seldom if ever catch colds, so it was unusual for me to be forced to see a doctor. After several visits to my GP and a year or so without a definite diagnosis, only changes to medication responding to increasing levels of pain, I was sent to a neurologist, who determined that I was suffering from trigeminal neuralgia and prescribed painkilling medication. This new medication helped somewhat, making the pain bearable enough that I was able to function daily.

That year, I wrote to my sons as follows:

I have been battling with trigeminal neuralgia, a condition that I am told by the neurologist I will have to live with. I believe it is caused by stress, or at least is aggravated by stress, so I am making sure that I get a lot of rest and eat properly. On bad days, even though it is only on the right side of my face and head, I can hardly brush my teeth, chew properly or comb my hair. ...

Since this is something I am told I have to live with, and in fact the doctor says it will get worse, with no proven medication ... I would be taking painkillers on a trial basis. I have decided to deal with this in a meditative way, that is, separate myself from the pain by literally ignoring it, or swearing at it, as best I can!

I took time to visit my son David and his family in Japan, fearing that with this condition I might not be able to go at a later time.

The *Levelling the Playing Field: Legacy of Vancouver's Asahi Baseball Team* exhibition was curated and opened soon after I returned from Japan in 2004, and I recall that as I was delivering the welcome speech to the crowd at the opening ceremony, I was hiding my red face under heavy makeup.

On one September morning, I drove to Jericho Beach. I sat against a log draped with a towel, reading an East Vancouver newspaper to take my mind off not only the pain but also the current museum situation I was not able to control. I hoped that sitting there, with the fresh air wafting over me and the hot sun rising, surrounded by squawking seagulls and the panoramic view stretching from Vancouver's tall buildings to North and West Vancouver's mountainsides to Spanish Banks, would calm my nerves.

My condition in the past few months had been the worst so far. The neurologist offered me nothing more, only a look of "That's it." I felt he was telling me, "Don't come to me for any more help. There's no cure for it; that is all we know." He offered no alternative solution, so I assumed I would have to live with this—and wondered if I could.

I had begun seeing a Sotai method practitioner, Koshi Ozeki, taking the advice of a friend who thought it might help. The sessions were strenuous, related to body alignment and easing muscular tensions, including heat therapy. They had no real effect on the trigeminal neuralgia, but at least this new experience motivated me to think of my physical and mental health. And so I had come to the beach for a couple of peaceful hours of meditation, taking in the sea air.

After a couple of hours of relaxing at the beach, I felt hungry. I longed to eat a hamburger or fish and chips or sushi, but I could hardly open my mouth since the pain shot down from my right temple behind my eye into my mouth with lightning speed if I tried.

I wondered how this could be happening to me, a food lover! I could only spoon tiny bits of food into the left side of my mouth, so soup, and porridge, which I hated, had moved to the top of my menu. I was worried about constipation, so with help from my very kind friend Vivien Nishi, I went to a store and bought a blender so I could mix various foods together to produce something healthy and edible. Vivien had earlier brought me a CD of uplifting Okinawan music, which I played loudly whenever I felt down (which was often).

Vivien found the address of a trigeminal neuralgia support group, and I contacted Ann Hopkins, who was the volunteer coordinator for Vancouver and the Lower Mainland. I attended a couple of meetings and Ann gave me some notes from a talk by the neurosurgeon Dr. Chris Honey, which helped me to understand what was happening to me. I was surprised to see many people attending these meetings.

I had initially been limited to two pills a day, but by the fall of 2006, as the pain grew excruciating, I was taking three a day and supplementing that with other pills. For someone like me, who had never taken pills, not even Aspirin, except once when I had the flu, it was perhaps a dangerous time, since I was no longer worried about dosage. I was no longer able to function between pain episodes and was forced to take time out from teaching Japanese-to-English translation to Japanese students two mornings a week, which I enjoyed.

Not wanting to miss the holidays with my grandchildren, I flew to Winnipeg for Christmas, as usual, to enjoy catching up with what my grandchildren were doing. The older two, Sarah and Samuel, were moving toward becoming barristers-at-law (following in the footsteps of both their father and their mother), and the youngest two, Isaac and Ava, were already showing signs of finding their own chosen paths.

My younger son and his family joined us by phone from Japan. Their son, my grandson Jamil, who was born and was being raised in Japan, would soon come to stay with me to attend Langara College.

Despite my condition, I felt blessed, having a family that I seldom if ever had reason to worry about but thought about every day with pride and joy. However, I could not eat the turkey dinner that I always looked forward to, prepared by my daughter-in-law Donna, with side dishes brought to the table by my sister Keiko and her husband, Art, and their family members. Michael and David's father, my ex-husband, as always joined us for Christmas dinner and holiday activities. It was a merry family gathering.

When I got back home to Vancouver at the beginning of January 2007, to make matters worse, I had lost my voice. There was no reason for this; I hadn't come down with the flu or anything else. I felt totally vulnerable, as I could not even call someone for help. Luckily, we live in the age of communication by email. So I let my dear friend Vivien know of my condition. She was immediately at my side, instantly taking over my life.

We discovered the neurologist was out of town for the holiday season. But, luckily, we were able to contact my GP, who put me on a new pain drug and also took another step of making an appointment for me with Dr. Gary Redekop, the head neurosurgeon at Vancouver General Hospital. This was the first time surgery had been mentioned as a possible solution.

I had lost a lot of weight by this time. I had not been eating properly. My GP sent me to see a nutritionist, who gave me information and guidelines about what I should be eating, calorie-wise, noting how little I had been taking in.

Without much optimism, I visited Dr. Redekop, supported by Vivien. He turned out to be a fairly young doctor. I was impressed with the way he greeted me and conducted the interview. The first step was to get an MRI done, he said, and he would get me an appointment within the next few days.

A young student/assistant interviewed me after I had met with the doctor, which I enjoyed. He asked me what I did, and I told him I was a retired curator of art exhibitions, more recently focused on Japanese Canadian history, but also had been teaching until the pain forced me to give it up. I admitted I was worried I might also have to stand down from the position of president of the National Association of Japanese Canadians, to which I had recently been elected.

After the MRI was done, I again met with Dr. Redekop, who, pointing to the screen, showed me exactly what was happening in my head, what was causing the pain, and the procedure to correct it. He said the surgery was 99 percent successful, and considering my good health to date, there should be no problem.

I had no hesitation about going ahead with the surgery. I had by this time even contemplated ending my life. I was blessed with a wonderful family and caring friends, and there were a few more things I wanted to do, but who would want to continue the life I was leading, controlled daily by pain?

When I awakened post-surgery, hearing the doctor telling me to touch my nose with my finger, the first words I spoke back to him were "I have no pain." It was unbelievable. Miraculous! From that day forward, as I tell my friends, I had become a bionic woman. As I understood it, a Teflon pad had been inserted between a nerve and the artery it had been rubbing against to cause the pain.

After close to five years of pain, I was finally healed. I later learned that my dear friends had been sitting in the hospital waiting room for several hours, awaiting the result of my surgery, and were happy to learn that all had gone well.

My son Michael had come from Winnipeg to give me support. He brought to my hospital room special food he had selected for me, every bite now possible to enjoy. Upon my return home from the hospital, he prepared a great dinner to celebrate the beginning of a new life for me and to offer thanks to my friends, especially Vivien, who had helped me through this long and painful period. My younger son, David, joined the celebration with a phone call from Japan.

And so I was reborn, ready to move on to new adventures.

COMMUNITY INVOLVEMENT

Soon after I had arrived in Vancouver in 1994 to my job as curator of the Burnaby Art Gallery, I had joined the board of the Greater Vancouver Japanese Canadian Citizens' Association. The main purpose was to become acquainted with the Japanese Canadian community of this area, where I had spent the earliest years of my life.

After leaving the Japanese Canadian National Museum position in 2002, I was elected to the executive board of the National Association of Japanese Canadians (NAJC). Two important issues came to our attention during this period.

One was the opening of the new Canadian War Museum in Ottawa in May 2005. Within weeks of the museum's move into its new building, the then president of the NAJC, Henry Kojima, was informed by surviving Japanese Canadian war veterans that on the floor devoted to the Second World War, which included a panel purportedly telling the story of Japanese Canadian internment, there was no mention of Japanese Canadians enlisting or participating in the First or Second World War.

As a board member of the NAJC, I visited the war museum and found the issue was not just omission but also misrepresentation of Japanese Canadian history. I made another visit, accompanied by an academic member of our community, also a war veteran, but when we received promises but no immediate action, I requested leadership from two respected members of our community, Dr. Ann Gomer Sunahara and Dr. Roy Miki. A position paper titled *Taking Responsibility: A Submission to the Canadian Government on the Misrepresentation of Japanese Canadians and Their History* was submitted to Prime Minister Stephen Harper and as a news release to the media in September 2010. Thanks to this effort, the museum quickly moved to make the changes as required, overseen to completion by Dr. Sunahara, who resides in

Ottawa. This paper is now filed with the Canadian government and is accessible to all.

Community vigilance, I found, is key to the preservation of our history.

The second issue that came to the NAJC executive board's attention was an announcement in September 2006 by Michael Fortier, minister of public works and government services, that a new office building at 401 Burrard Street in downtown Vancouver was to be named in honour of former cabinet minister Howard Green.

There is no doubt that as a cabinet minister during the John Diefenbaker era, Mr. Green had distinguished himself. In citing his background of service, particularly as secretary of state for external affairs between 1959 and 1963, Prime Minister Harper referred to Mr. Green as "one of the greatest leaders in the field of disarmament and world peace," someone with achievements "in the field of international affairs and the pursuit of peace for all mankind."

What was forgotten or ignored by the prime minister was that, from the 1930s into the 1940s, Mr. Green, joined by BC and Vancouver politicians, had engaged in relentless fear mongering against Japanese Canadians. His shrill voice is well documented in newspaper articles and headlines of this period. Mr. Green may have distinguished himself during the postwar years, but he had never offered the Japanese Canadian community a word of apology for his role in advocating internment and the deportation of people of Japanese ancestry, or for speaking against the return of Japanese Canadians to the West Coast.

Henry Kojima, in a letter to Minister Fortier dated October 4, 2006, commented, "It is the height of irony that the Conservative Government of Prime Minister Brian Mulroney in 1988 rose in Parliament and apologized to Canadians of Japanese ancestry for the injustices and discrimination perpetuated against our community in British Columbia prior to and during the Second World War. In 2006, the same Conservative Government is now honouring one of the influential British Columbia leaders of that time for the part he played in the tragic history of our country."[7]

---

7   Letter from Henry Kojima to Minister Michael Fortier, October 4, 2006, National Association of Japanese Canadians head office, Winnipeg.

In response to the NAJC's request for reconsideration, Mr. Fortier's selection committee reconvened in December 2006. Presentations against naming the building after Howard Green were made to the selection committee by Dr. Roy Miki, a distinguished academic, a poet and the author of *Redress: Inside the Japanese Canadian Call for Justice*; Keiko Mary Kitagawa, representing the Greater Vancouver Japanese Canadian Citizens' Association's Human Rights Committee; and myself, now president of the National Association of Japanese Canadians.

On September 7, 2007, at an official naming ceremony, the building was renamed Douglas Jung Building, honouring the first Chinese Canadian Member of Parliament. Mr. Jung represented the riding of Vancouver Centre from 1957 to 1962 as a Progressive Conservative.

Also noteworthy was the celebration of the twentieth anniversary of Japanese Canadian Redress, held in Vancouver September 19–21, 2008. As NAJC president, I had the pleasure of organizing the event, along with many community members and national volunteers, and with staff assistant Cindy Mochizuki. Diverse programs were planned for various venues, including the Vancouver Japanese Language School and Japanese Hall on Alexander Street, and Nikkei Place and the Alan Emmott Centre in Burnaby. Generous funding support was received from both public and private sources. Workshops on such themes as history, human rights, migration, community health and intercultural issues were held throughout the weekend at these appointed sites.

Both documentary and art videos were screened. Music and dance performances were held between workshops. Vancouver-based Kokoro Dance, led by Barbara Bourget and Jay Hirabayashi, performed a forty-five-minute, site-specific piece on a rooftop of a Downtown Eastside building. This new work revisited the history that had produced the company's shows *Rage*, in 1987, and *The Believer*, in 1995. The latter was developed as a touring school program.

The celebration was topped with a large banquet at the Nikkei Centre, attended not only by the participating national Japanese Canadian community organizational members and friends but also by representatives from the city, the provincial government and the federal government, as well as the visiting Japanese ambassador and the local consul general.

Our respected guest Robert Joseph, Hereditary Chief of the Gwawaenuk First Nation and a residential school survivor, offered a memorable closing speech. Chief Joseph spoke about his commitment, through the Indigenous-led organization Reconciliation Canada, to bringing together all people for a deeper dialogue about reconciliation and talked about how we can all reach into our souls for a profound and sustainable understanding. (The Truth and Reconciliation Commission of Canada had been established by the Government of Canada that year.)

ᕕᖬᕗ

When the City of Vancouver in 2013 offered to make an apology to Japanese Canadians for the city's role in the uprooting of Japanese Canadians in 1942, I, as one of the few survivors of this history, was invited to speak to the motion on behalf of the Greater Vancouver Japanese Canadian Citizens' Association's Human Rights Committee. A "sorry" at this late date from current city council members would have little meaning, I felt, so at first I was hesitant to accept this "honour."

(At this time I knew little about the Vancouver City Council's role in the decision-making process vis-à-vis the federal government's orders in the 1940s, especially the confiscation and sale of all personal property forcibly left behind by Japanese Canadians, or in the later decision not to allow those of Japanese ancestry to return to the West Coast, even after the war had ended.)

Upon reading the draft wording of the apology, I made a special request to add a further pledge: that the city would "do all it can to ensure such injustices will not happen again to any of its residents."

This additional pledge was, I felt, necessary to the future of the city of Vancouver. Today, residents of Vancouver's Downtown Eastside neighbourhood are contending with rapid gentrification by developers, with city approval becoming the norm. Rentals have become unaffordable for most of the neighbourhood's residents, with the number of homeless people increasing by the day.

I was pleased when the city council accepted and extended the wording of this new pledge, adding the phrase "thereby upholding the principles of human rights, justice and equality now and in the future."

Councillor Kerry Jang, who had championed the apology to Japanese Canadians, assured us then that the Downtown Eastside Local Area Planning Process would ensure the future of the neighbourhood. Only time will tell if the pledge will be honoured by future city council members so that all Vancouver residents are kept safe, not displaced, just as Japanese Canadians and, earlier, the original Coast Salish Indigenous Peoples were displaced, racism being the root cause.

At the time this book was written (2018), there were some 2,000 homeless people in the city of Vancouver. At many corners on the city's busy streets, people can be seen sitting or standing on the sidewalk asking for help. Sadly, we live in a world in which the middle class is shrinking and poverty is increasing, while a small percentage of the rich grab most of the revenue.

✑

What gives me hope and excites me most today is that a significant number of younger people, the fourth and fifth generations and beyond, now largely of mixed ethnicities and heritage, are taking interest in their ancestral histories. Many grew up without knowledge of their roots, particularly the history of displacements.

Young and older people within the Japanese Canadian community, together with other locals, volunteer in the production of the annual Powell Street Festival, held since 1977. Commemorating Japanese Canadians' early settlement in Paueru Gai and the uprooting of our community in 1942, the festival, with traditional and contemporary performances and displays, draws a mixed crowd of tens of thousands to Vancouver's Downtown Eastside over the August long weekend.

Following the Powell Street Festival each year is the Vancouver Asahi Tribute Game. The tenth annual event in 2018, held on the former Powell Ground (now Oppenheimer Park), was advertised as follows (written on behalf of the Powell Street Festival Society by Angela Kruger):

The Vancouver Asahi was a Japanese Canadian baseball team that played in the Powell Street area, a historically Japanese

Canadian community, from 1914 to 1941. Their home field was Oppenheimer Park.

We play baseball in recognition of the Vancouver Asahi for their contribution to the sport of baseball (the team was inducted into the Canadian Baseball Hall of Fame in 2003 and the BC Sports Hall of Fame in 2005), and for their place in and impact on the history of Canada, human and citizenship rights, and community-building.

The 10th Annual Vancouver Asahi Tribute Game is a free, inclusive and family-friendly place to play ball, eat hot dogs, and come together for some summer fun!

Through my research of this team's history, leading to the 2004 *Levelling the Playing Field* exhibition at the Japanese Canadian National Museum, I had come to be considered an "expert" on this subject (though hardly true), and I continue to be invited to speak at public events whenever the story of the Asahi comes into play.

I have had the honour of being consulted in connection with several film productions about the team, most recently by Historica Canada's

The Vancouver Asahi team, established in Paueru Gai from 1914 to 1941, is remembered and celebrated each year at the Powell Street Festival with a tribute game in Oppenheimer Park. Nikkei National Museum; 2011-78-10

Heritage Minute celebrating the 100th anniversary of the Asahi's first league championship in 1919.

Another opportunity to preserve this history came earlier when I read the Japanese sportscaster Norio Goto's book, *Vancouver Asahi Monogatari*, published in 2010 by Iwanami Shoten in Japan. What interested me about this book was that it was, yes, about baseball, but most importantly about a team that persevered to overcome obstacles, through a strategy that came to be known as "brain ball," during a period when the Asahi players and their families were dealing daily with racial discrimination in all aspects of their lives. Such a book, I decided, might arouse interest among younger generations. It took a few years, but I sought permission from the writer and the publisher to publish an English translation of the book here in Canada. There was much interest among our national Japanese Canadian communities, and I received enough private and individual donations to cover the translation fee, with initial support from the Japanese Canadian Studies Society as sponsor.

Even though I found an excellent translator, Masaki Watanabe, this was not an easy project I had undertaken. I was pleased during the process to be joined by Elmer Morishita, a baseball enthusiast and a great administrator. We moved forward to the second stage of fundraising, for the printing and publishing costs (covered by a small circle of friends), and we were finally able to launch the English-language edition of this book in 2016, under the title *Story of Vancouver Asahi: A Legend in Baseball.*

This accomplishment is one I feel very proud of, as the English-language book is now being read by both young and older people here in Canada, just as I had hoped. We offered a copy as a gift to each teenaged member of the Shin (New) Asahi team so that they might understand this heritage as they prepared for a trip to Japan in 2019. (The book is currently being sold by the Nikkei National Museum & Cultural Centre gift shop in Burnaby.)

During production of the 2014 Japanese film *Bankūbā no Asahi* (*The Vancouver Asahi*), the Japanese crew, including the producer and the director of the film, visited and consulted with us here in Canada.

The film was directed by an award-winning Japanese director, Yuya Ishii (best known for his movie *The Great Passage*, for which he won best director at the 2013 Japanese Academy Awards).

The film had its world premiere at the Vancouver International Film Festival in September 2014. In his response to my correspondence with him more recently regarding the planning of the movie, Mr. Ishii said it was a "big challenge" for him, "a contemporary Japanese, to take on a pre-war Nisei narrative." He had received much advice from many of us here in Canada, particularly from Mr. Kaye Kaminishi, the only Asahi player remaining today. After much investigation into the limits of possibility in telling this story, Mr. Ishii said, what emerged for him was the importance of the Asahi spirit—not merely introducing the history of the Asahi, but "the spirit is what I decided. For that reason it became a universal story. Not only for Nikkei and global minorities ... no, more than that ... also, for people like myself ... it became a movie to be transmitted strongly. In order to make a movie into a universal one, strength of fiction is what I used. ... It is not just about baseball, but to know the spirit of the Asahi, to feel this ... I want the audience to feel more deeply the ... emotions."

He added that he was very happy to have had the opportunity to make this film. "I feel very grateful. This film is not only for Japan ... but worldwide people's response is what I am hoping for."

And that is what has happened. More and more people internationally are learning and speaking about this extraordinary team and its time in history, here in Canada.

⟨⟩

Another Downtown Eastside event I was introduced to around 2008 was the Heart of the City Festival. Once I learned about this festival from Terry Hunter and Savannah Walling, executive director and artistic director, respectively, of the Vancouver Moving Theatre, I began attending performances that still remain within me.

One was *Bread and Salt*, a heart-rending story told by Ukrainian community performers about the struggles of early European immigrants to Canada, including the First World War internment of Ukrainians. Having met and made friends with members of the large

Ukrainian Canadian community in Winnipeg, I took a special interest in learning about this past, relating their emotional experiences to my own memories of the Japanese Canadian internment.

(In June 2015, I was asked by Dr. Rhonda Hinther of Brandon University in Manitoba to take part in a workshop titled "Civilian Internment in Canada: Histories and Legacies," held at the Ukrainian Labour Temple hall in Winnipeg. I was invited to offer a personal account of the Japanese Canadian internment through participation in panel discussions, but I was also asked to submit a paper of this experience. This submission began my process of seriously reconsidering Mother's memoir, not only to be translated and offered to family members but also to add my own memories alongside hers. Dr. Hinther tells me that articles, materials and testimonials from the workshop participants will be pulled together as a publication that will offer "multiple perspectives on internment from a variety of communities that experienced it.")

After watching another Vancouver Moving Theatre performance, *Storyweaving*, in 2012, with its "weaving" of memories and stories from the past into the future, I was moved enough to write a short piece in the Greater Vancouver Japanese Canadian Citizens' Association's monthly *Bulletin*, edited by John Endo Greenaway, about my response:

> Today, we acknowledge the injustices perpetrated on the First Nations communities and individuals ... and are aware more particularly of events, such as the Indian Residential Schools Settlement Agreement, Missing Women's Commission Inquiry, and the Truth and Reconciliation Commission Community Hearings, which are finally working at dealing with longstanding issues. ...
>
> But there is no doubt also that many among us grew up in a Canada which offered biased interpretations of First Nations' histories and colonization ... which have only very recently in this history begun to include the viewpoints of First Nations' experience and memories. Such mythologizing of peoples induced generations of Canadians to marginalize on the basis of "difference."

So it was that I sat as one of the audience at this performance and, halfway through, found myself weeping. While
I tried, I couldn't stop weeping. I was not alone. All around
me, men and women were blowing their noses and wiping
tears from their eyes. ... The script is not a play script but a
real life script, felt and grieved by each of the performers,
who with spiritual and bodily languages and with great faith
and courage and optimism fight the fight, knowing they are
succeeding.[8]

Why was I crying, amid all this optimism and courage? Was it feelings
of guilt? What had I done in my lifetime to show I cared about the
conditions under which First Nations communities were living, are living, to this day? I had lived my life self-centredly dealing with my own
issues of identity, of belonging to a community and to a family that
was racialized. When, during the performance, the White Lunch was
remembered as a restaurant on the east side that had a sign to keep out
"Natives," this struck a chord in me, as I recalled my father telling me
that "Orientals" were not allowed entry to this café.

Over the past twenty-five years, my research into Japanese Canadian history, that is, my own heritage, led me to speak out on cross-cultural human rights issues, to the end that no one and no group should
ever be treated the way some communities were. We must each of us
take responsibility to stay vigilant and to work toward a better Canada
for everyone.

In 2015, I was invited to participate in the Vancouver Moving
Theatre production *Against the Current*. A cross-cultural production,
it opened with a Coast Salish welcome song from the musician and
composer Russell Wallace of the group Tzo'kam, followed by a procession of dancers and drummers, including the Fishstix group. The show
was developed in partnership with the Vancouver Taiko Society and other
groups, including Vancouver Okinawa Taiko, with John Endo Greenaway
as artistic director and Rosemary Georgeson, a Coast Salish and Sahtu

---

8   Grace Eiko Thomson, "My Response to Storyweaving," *Bulletin*, June 14, 2012.

Dene artist, writer and storyteller and recipient of a 2009 Vancouver Mayor's Arts Award, as the Indigenous narrator.

The one-evening production featuring sixty performers was held at the Vancouver Japanese Language School and Japanese Hall. The title *Against the Current* refers to the journey of returning salmon upstream, a metaphor for the difficult journeys of survival experienced by Indigenous and Japanese Canadian fishers along the west coast of British Columbia.

I was honoured to participate as a narrator of poetic lines written by John Endo Greenaway, representing Japanese Canadian fisher experiences, to accompany the main narration by Rosemary Georgeson. I offer a few lines below (courtesy of Vancouver Moving Theatre):

Grace:
Ascending rivers from the sea
to breed, upstream
transforming
silver to crimson
chinook, coho, sockeye, chum, pink ...
Swimming up fifty salmon-bearing streams
Flooding down gullies
Onto False Creek and the Fraser River,
Spilling into salt-water tidal flats.

Rosemary:
"When the tide is out, the table is set,"
Said Coast Salish Peoples.
Nourished by these lands and waters
Since time immemorial,
Coast Salish people have been
seeking salmon with fish weirs,
Spears and stinging nettle nets.
Thank you salmon people,
Thank you for sending the salmon.
"Salmon Bones, return to the sea.
Bring new salmon, year after year after year."

Thus begins the play, with the following explanation by Rosemary:

Today we stand on unceded Coast Salish Territory. Hastings Reserve.

Nihonmachi. The Downtown Eastside. In the Japanese Hall.

Living monuments stand on the land, cedar and cherry trees

Memorials honour those we have lost and those who have survived.

Today ... In Paueru Groundo. Oppenheimer Park. Community backyard.

Gathering place for

Coast Salish, urban Aboriginal,

Japanese Canadian, Latino,

Immigrants from the four directions

And those seeking sanctuary.

A gathering place for memories.

Ancestral Voices.

The play ends with a message: "May you multiply and return forever."
   The appreciation expressed by the large cross-cultural audience affirmed the incredible power of art, especially when it is produced in cross-cultural collaboration, in trust and with love and passion, based on our histories. It was a privilege and an honour for me to have been invited to take part.

In 2014, members of Vancouver's diverse communities who had survived discrimination and atrocities—such as the Chinese head tax, the Japanese Canadian internment, the displacement of the Black community from Hogan's Alley and the 1914 *Komagata Maru* incident in which passengers who had travelled from India were detained in Vancouver Harbour—gathered, together with current Downtown Eastside residents facing issues of gentrification, at the Sacred Circle Society on West Cordova Street to discuss human rights struggles. The outcome of these gatherings was the decision to raise a totem pole to symbolize resistance, persistence and inclusion.

The totem pole was carved by Skundaal Bernie Williams (Gul Kitt Jaad) of the Coast Salish and Haida Peoples, who was raised by her grandmother Nonnie Agnes Williams. Skundaal is a survivor of the residential school system. The mother of three sons and grandmother of six, she has been working in the Downtown Eastside for some thirty years.

As the only female apprentice of the late Haida artist Bill Reid, Skundaal had carved twelve previous totem poles, but this one, she says, had special meaning for her. Her mother and sisters were among the many missing and murdered Indigenous women, and she told the *Georgia Straight* that her Survivors' Totem Pole "is for everybody: it represents the resilience of everyone who has faced racism, colonialism, sexism, LGBTQ-bashing, gentrification, and more. These things have really affected this whole community. We want to let people that are moving into this area know that this is a great community, that we are still part of it, and we're not going away. We are here to stay, and this pole is a lasting legacy for these people, and all the people that have helped make this happen."[9]

Audrey Siegl, a board member of the Sacred Circle Society and a Musqueam activist, told the *Straight* in the same article that "much of what has occurred in the [Downtown Eastside] comes down to one thing: the continued prioritization, by all levels of government, of

---

9   Amanda Siebert, "Bernie Williams's Survivors' Totem Pole Will Be a Symbol of Hope for Residents of the Downtown Eastside," *Georgia Straight*, November 3, 2016.

dollars over life. 'The end result is that everybody loses. This pole is a win-win,'" she said.

A poem by the late Sandy Cameron, a long-time activist and community member, offered by his life partner, Jean Swanson, an anti-poverty activist and Vancouver city councillor, is engraved at the base of the totem pole:

> Sing your song, friend.
> Tell your story.
> The map we inherited
> Isn't any good.
> The old roads mislead.
> We need a new map.

On November 5, 2016, community members carried the pole down Hastings Street in a procession to its new home in the heart of the Downtown Eastside (DTES), Pigeon Park, at Carrall and Hastings Streets. In a ceremony featuring drumming, dancing and regalia, the pole was carefully lifted into position by a crane.

Project partners included the City of Vancouver, the Portland Hotel Society, the Potluck Café and the Vancouver Moving Theatre/Heart of the City Festival.

I totally agree with the comments of hope made at the event by Gregor Robertson, then mayor of Vancouver, who participated in witnessing the ceremony with hundreds of others: "My wish is that this place, where the totem is raised, will be used not only as a place for meditation, but also as an education centre, particularly for the new generations of students who know little about this history (or about current DTES issues), and I encourage public school systems to include such stories in their curriculum. With such knowledge leading to changes, we can look with courage to move forward to a better future."[10]

(The filmmaker Susanne Tabata has documented both the lead-up to the pole installation and the historic pole-raising day.)

---

10   "Mayor's Words," *Georgia Straight*, November 5, 2016.

I would like to end my memoir remembering Chief Robert Joseph's ending speech at the NAJC twentieth anniversary celebration in 2008. Following our first meeting of that weekend, I was honoured as an elder by Reconciliation Canada and named as one of its ambassadors, later blanketed together with several others at a special ceremony in 2017. In his own way, Chief Joseph, affectionately called Chief Bobby Jo, by holding community circles provincially and nationally and inviting everyone to join hands with him, taught me that reconciliation, a goal I had earlier doubted was possible, must begin firstly within oneself.

At the three-day circle workshops Chief Joseph led, I was inspired, listening to stories offered by others and sharing my own. In time, with community assistance, together with Lucille Wang of the Chinese Canadian community and others, we produced our own fifty-person circle at the Vancouver Buddhist Temple. The circle brought together people from the Downtown Eastside's various communities, including several members of the Japanese Canadian community.

Many who took part in the workshop, often with tears streaming down their cheeks, shared their own stories. At the end of the event, from which no one was excluded, the word most often heard from the participants as they were leaving was "amazing."

The Reconciliation Canada poster offers the message "Namwayut: We are all one."

I have learned, through the long journey of seeking resolution, that we are indeed *all one*. It is up to us, each one of us, to ensure *justice for all*.

I recall Mother evoking at the end of her memoir the haiku by Master Ryōkan: the significance of *chiru sakura*, that is, the falling *sakura* (cherry blossoms), as she reached the last years of her own life. I will close my memoir, with optimism for the future, for my family and friends, with *saku sakura* (blooming *sakura*).

Sakura in bloom
Announces spring's arrival
Keeping hopes alive

PHOTO GALLERY

Nishikihama family, Mother, Father, Eiko (Grace), Toyoaki (Tom), Kenji, and Keiko, leaving Minto in response to the government's dispersal order to move to the east of the Rockies, 1944. Neighbour, Mrs. Nishi and her daughter, Namiko bidding goodbye.

Grace's father (left), and Uncle Konosuke (right), with friends, upon arrival at Minto Mine's hotel, 1942.

Street photo of Grace's brother, Tom (Toyoaki) Nishikihama, walking in downtown Vancouver, c. 1956.

Mother's first visit to Japan post-internment, 1962, with friends on a scenic tour.

Grace touring in Kyoto, where she was invited to speak at Nishi Honganji's Fifth Gathering for Peace, held in Shiga Prefecture, in Japan, December 2003.

Grace exploring the back streets of Tokyo, 2016.

REFERENCES AND SUGGESTED READING

The following list includes sources for the historical information in this book as well as references I have read through the years, adding to my own memories of this period in our history.

Japanese Canadian History

Adachi, Ken. *The Enemy That Never Was: A History of Japanese Canadians*. Toronto: McClelland & Stewart, 1976.

Ito, Roy. *The Japanese Canadians*. Multicultural Canada Series. Toronto: Van Nostrand Reinhold, 1992.

Johnson, Genevieve Fuji, and Randy Enomoto, eds. *Race, Racialization and Antiracism in Canada and Beyond*. Toronto: University of Toronto Press, 2007.

Kess, Joseph F., Hiroko Noro, Midge M. Ayukawa, and Helen Lansdowne, eds. *Changing Japanese Identities in Multicultural Canada*. Victoria: University of Victoria, 2003.

Kitagawa, Muriel. *This Is My Own: Letters to Wes and Other Writings on Japanese Canadians, 1941–1948*. Edited by Roy Miki. Vancouver: Talonbooks, 1985.

Kobayashi, Cassandra, and Roy Miki, eds. *Spirit of Redress: Japanese Canadians in Conference*. Vancouver: JC Publications, 1989.

Kobayashi, Teiji, ed. *35 Years of History of the Steveston Fishermen's Benevolent Society*. 2013. Bill McNulty collection, Nikkei National Museum. English translation of Japanese text.

Makabe, Tomoko. *Picture Brides: Japanese Women in Canada*. Translated by Kathleen Chisato Merken. Toronto: Multicultural History Society of Ontario, 1995.

Manitoba Japanese Canadian Citizens' Association. *The History of Japanese Canadians in Manitoba*. Winnipeg: Manitoba Japanese Canadian Citizens' Association, 1996.

McAllister, Kirsten Emiko. *Terrain of Memory: A Japanese Canadian Memorial Project*. Vancouver: UBC Press, 2010.

Miki, Roy. *Redress: Inside the Japanese Canadian Call for Justice*. Vancouver: Raincoast Books, 2004.

Miki, Roy, and Cassandra Kobayashi. *Justice in Our Time: The Japanese Canadian Redress Settlement*. Vancouver: Talonbooks, 1991. (Includes Prime Minister Brian Mulroney's acknowledgement and the Japanese Canadian Redress Agreement.)

Moritsugu, Frank, and Ghost-Town Teachers Historical Society. *Teaching in Canadian Exile: A History of the Schools for Japanese-Canadian Children in British Columbia Detention Camps during the Second World War*. Toronto: Ghost-Town Teachers Historical Society, 2001.

Oikawa, Mona. *Cartographies of Violence: Japanese Canadian Women, Memory, and the Subjects of the Internment*. Toronto: University of Toronto Press, 2012.

Shimizu, Kosaburo. *Kosaburo Shimizu: The Early Diaries, 1909–1926*. Translated by Tsuguo Arai. Edited by Grace Arai. Anchorage: AT Publishing, 2005.

Japanese Canadian Military History

Broadfoot, Barry. *Years of Sorrow, Years of Shame: The Story of the Japanese Canadians in World War II*. Toronto: PaperJacks, 1977.

Dick, Lyle. "Sergeant Masumi Mitsui and the Japanese Canadian War Memorial: Intersections of National, Cultural, and Personal Memory." *Canadian Historical Review* 91, no. 3 (September 2010): 435–63.

Greenaway, John Endo. "They Went to War: Japanese Canadians and the Battle for Acceptance." *Bulletin* (Greater Vancouver Japanese Canadian Citizens' Association), November 9, 2013.

Ito, Roy. *We Went to War: The Story of the Japanese Canadians Who Served during the First and Second World Wars*. Etobicoke, ON: S-20 and Nisei Veterans Association, 1984.

Oki, Jack. "The Canadian Nisei Veteran's Story." *New Canadian*, December 27, 1967.

Wakayama, Tamio. "Lest We Forget: A Dedication to Commemorate the Re-lighting of the War Memorial to Japanese Canadian Soldiers of World War I, August 2, 1985." *Nikkei Images* 10, no. 3 (Autumn 2005): 5–7.

Exhibition Catalogues

Reshaping Memory, Owning History: Through the Lens of Japanese Canadian Redress. Burnaby: Japanese Canadian National Museum, 2000. Curated by Grace Eiko Thomson.

Shashin: Japanese Canadian Photography to 1942. Burnaby: Japanese Canadian National Museum, 2004. Curated by Grace Eiko Thomson.

Separate Identities: Sharing Worlds. Prince Albert, SK: Little Gallery; Regina, SK: MacKenzie Art Gallery, 1993. Curated by Bob Boyer.

Acknowledgements

I will begin by thanking my respected activist friends, Rita Wong and Lily Yuri Shinde, who introduced me to the editor of note, Barbara Pulling. She, upon editing the first draft, very generously offered me time and advice, suggesting I seek a publisher instead of self-publishing which was my first intent. Her encouragement and belief in this story gave me the courage to think of my memoir in a different way.

Sincere gratitude goes to Vici Johnstone, Publisher, Caitlin Press, who very generously accepted without hesitation, which offered me much encouragement. Through the process, I was introduced to Meg Yamamoto, Monica Miller, and Sarah Corsie. I thank them all, very much!

Special thanks go to family members: my two sons, Michael Andrew Thomson (a Court of Queen's Bench Judge, Winnipeg), and David Alexander Thomson (who runs an English-language school in Japan); their father, Alistair Macdonald Thomson; and five wonderful grandchildren and their very special mothers. I acknowledge also, my younger sister, Keiko, and her family, as well, my older sister Kikuko's three children—her daughter Brenda, my niece, lives here in Vancouver.

Most importantly, I acknowledge my Mother, whose memoir inspired me to document my own memories alongside hers. Thank you, Mother.

ABOUT THE AUTHOR

Grace Eiko Thomson is a second-generation Japanese Canadian who, with her parents and siblings, lived in Paueru Gai (Powell Street, Downtown Eastside) in Vancouver until 1942, when they were sent to the internment site of Minto Mines, BC, then in 1945 to rural Manitoba. After restrictions were lifted, they re-settled in the City of Winnipeg (1950).

Grace's education focused on her need to overcome memories of racism and identity issues, through investigation of her cultural roots and through art. She graduated from University of Manitoba (BFA Hons. 1973-77), and University of Leeds, UK, (M. Soc. History of Art, 1990-91).

As curator of various art galleries (1983-98), she concentrated on cross-cultural issues as well as women's issues. In 2000, as Director/Curator, she launched the Japanese Canadian National Museum. She was President of the National Association of Japanese Canadians in 2008 and served on the National Executive Board from 2005 to 2010. She is mother to two sons and grandmother to five grandchildren, and currently participates in various Downtown Eastside activities and issues.